"There's a saying that every p⸻ ⸻idden Treasures you will be invited ⸻ ⸻ Chan's life story. At times, you'll need to p⸻ ⸻at you're reading. At other times, you'll want to s⸻ ⸻eading to find out what happened. This story is one of ⸻ ⸻ering hope, even in the most hopeless circumstances.

It was a privilege to work with Kit Ying before, during, and after the events recorded in Nanning. She will always be one we honor and esteem for who she is and what she's allowed to happen through her life."

Gary & Helen Stephens, co-founders of Mother's Choice,
author of Waiting for a Father

"Kit Ying has dedicated her life to improving the welfare of children. As the founder of Mother's Love in China, and through her ongoing work for orphans she has been a witness to history. Telling her story will help make connections and answer lingering questions of adopted children about their own journeys."

Jian Chen, Vice President – China, Holt International

"It was my real privilege to have the opportunity to collaborate with Kit Ying in Guangxi over 20 years ago. At that time, China was in the process of opening up and was challenged by extreme demand for orphan care under the one-child policy. During my many personal visits to the Mother's Love home, I witnessed the tender loving care of every staff towards those babies abandoned by men, yet cherished and precious in the eyes of God and those who knew Him. It was nothing short of a miracle that such acts of Christian charity persevered for well over two decades in Nanning. I believe that everyone who came to know this ministry was blessed and changed for the better."

Dr. Thomas Chan, Chairman of the Board,
World Vision China Foundation

"When I heard Kit Ying had written a book about her experience with starting Mother's Love, I could not have been more excited. Her love for children and her desire to provide them with love and dignity compelled her to action, and that action, in turn, made an enormous difference in the lives of so many. This story is interwoven with heartbreak, but it is moving and hopeful and is a great testimony to the fact that one person, with God's help, can set in motion changes that will make a lifelong impact. Kit Ying truly has a heart of gold, and I'm thrilled she's provided this opportunity for her readers, and particularly for the children whom she cared for during her time in Guangxi, to know the history and stories behind her efforts to make a difference and to provide hope in the midst of challenging times."

Cheung-Ang Siew Mei JP, Executive Director, Christian Action

"I had the unforgettable privilege visiting Mother's Love and meeting with Kit Ying in the fall of 1998. The caring and loving environment she single-handedly built for abandoned girls was truly a little heaven on earth. The unsurmountable hardship she overcame to rescue each precious life from the mouth of death was monumental. I walked away saying to myself: She is the Mother Teresa of China!

The Hidden Treasures offers a telescopic and powerful true story of Kit Ying saving 1,5000 abandoned children and impacting many thousands more across China as a result of her child care model — Mother's Love. This book demonstrates what amazing things one can accomplish when we are willing to be used by God."

Joshua Zhong, Co-founder & President
of Chinese Children Charities

HIDDEN
TREASURES

A Letter to the Children of
Mother's Love, Guangxi, China

Thanks for modelling Father God to so many children who need His love!

Kit Ying

2019' Hong Kong

KIT YING CHAN

with Richard Balme,
Jennifer Cheng & Serrie Fung

This book is dedicated to
the children of Mother's Love & their forever families,
including all the babies & children
who didn't make it on earth,
and have gone to their eternal home.

Child care workers and children at Mother's Love, 1997.

Contents

Foreword

Kit Ying to me is the embodiment of everything that I admire: service, love, duty, and humility. In her life and her work, she has exemplified all these attributes to the fullest, that have not only seen her overcome extreme obstacles, but has inspired us all.

For more than three decades, Kit Ying has been associated with Mother's Choice, a unique organization that was set up to support pregnant teenagers who had nowhere else to turn. In the years following, this non-judgmental service began to include care for the children who were abandoned and uncared for, and took her to China, where she began her work with Chinese state orphanages. In 1995, Kit Ying founded the first joint venture between Hong Kong and China and the Guangxi-Hong Kong Mother's Love Orphanage was created.

Dr. Rosanna Wong at the Mother's Love 10th anniversary celebrations in 2005.

My memories of these early days were Kit Ying's relentless energy and passion to succeed in spite of all the hurdles in front of her. Her determination to pioneer a professional model for child care, fostering, and specialized care for children with special needs, built a foundation on which China's efforts can only develop and progress.

Mother's Love no longer exists. However, every child who passed through its doors felt Kit Ying's love and had all her hopes imbued in their lives. They are now young adults, scattered around the world, who literally and figuratively owe their start to Kit Ying.

Hidden Treasures is that story. It is a true story of the power of love and service, and how with both, everything and anything is possible.

It has been my honor and privilege to have been a very small part of this journey, and as we celebrate Mother's Love and Kit Ying, I am again reminded of the words of St. Paul, which capture the spirit of this wonderful book and this amazing woman:

"And now these three remain: faith, hope and love. But the greatest of these is love." – 1 Corinthians 13:13

Dr. Rosanna Wong, DBE, JP
Vice Patron and Ambassador
Mother's Choice

Preface

"The kingdom of heaven is like treasure hidden in a field. When a man found it, he hid it again, and then in his joy went and sold all he had and bought that field." – Matthew 13:44

The beginning of the 1990s was a time of enormous economic and social progress in the People's Republic of China, resulting in drastically improved conditions in employment, income, housing, health, and education. However, this rapid pace of change also came with a slew of challenges. One of those challenges was what later became known as the baby abandonment crisis of the 1990s that resulted from the country's one-child policy. Reports in international media outlets exposed the terrible conditions in the state orphanages that struggled to keep up with the overwhelming numbers of abandoned baby girls across China. In 1992, when I was sent to the Nanning state orphanage to conduct a needs assessment, I had no idea that I would come face-to-face with this crisis, and that the scenes that I saw would call me to leave my life in Hong Kong and move to Nanning.

As the world came to hear about the crisis unfolding in China, increasing numbers of foreign aid workers and missionaries arrived to help rescue the babies, and as international adoption was introduced in China, families in the West opened up their hearts and their homes to adopt many of these children. For those who were adopted, details of their life prior to adoption are often vague at best, and information about their origins and the identities of their birth parents is mostly non-existent. The ability to track whatever scraps of information that are available is made all the more difficult with the barriers of time, distance, and language. The journey of discovery can also raise complex questions: What difficult information might we be confronted with? How will this impact bonds within the family? How will each party react emotionally? These are challenging questions, with no simple answers.

A few years ago, around Christmas 2012, a translator in Nanning who served adoptees and their families returning to China for 'homeland visits' introduced me to a beautiful young lady who I remembered as baby Fei Kang. Her adoptive mother reminded me that Fei Kang had been on the brink of death when I found her and started caring for her. Fei Kang was adopted to the US in 1995, and now Faith Ann, at 19, had bravely traveled to Guangxi entirely on her own in search for her heritage. We spent Christmas together in Nanning, and I invited her to spend a week with me in Hong Kong before flying back home to the US.

Faith Ann and me, Christmas 2012.

This week together was precious for both of us as I tried my best to share with Faith Ann the history of China, my years in Nanning, and many stories of Mother's Love. We looked through old photos together and watched a video taken from my first trip to the Nanning state orphanage. As emotions unfolded while we watched, she quietly leaned closer to me and put her head on my shoulder. I held her close while we finished watching the video.

In that moment, it became clear to me that it was essential that I put these children's stories and their shared history into a book. As parents typically pass a legacy onto their children, I recognized that I also had the responsibility to share with these thousands of children and their families what I could about their past. The building where Mother's Love lived was destroyed, falling victim to urban development between 2012 and 2014. The people who were involved in Mother's Love have dispersed over the years (though many of them continue to stay in contact). With the passing of time, and as the physical remnants of what happened in Nanning in the 1900s and 2000s slowly fade, it is ever more important for me to tell this story so that there is a record of what happened for adoptees to find when they are ready. I want to assure each of the adoptees that although the physical building of Mother's Love no longer exists, the legacy of Mother's Love continues to live on with those who were involved, in the very lives of the adoptees, wherever they may be now.

This book is written for them, the children of Nanning, Guangxi, China, particularly those fostered by and adopted during my first few years at the Nanning state orphanage in 1992-1994 and subsequently through Mother's Love in 1995-2011. I particularly think of those who will not have the opportunity to travel to Nanning.

In writing this book, I have tried to include as many details as possible about how and why Mother's Love started. There are, however, some questions for which there are simply no answers—particularly surrounding the specific identity and situations of the individual parents who abandoned their babies. Seeing firsthand the situation in China at the time, I can however testify to the desperation behind so many children being abandoned in the 1990s. Causes of mass abandonment do not stand with the poor morality or lack of affection of biological parents, but with the social, economic, and political conditions making it impossible for them to choose otherwise.

Through reading this book, I want adoptees to know that in spite of the reality their abandonment, they were fiercely loved by myself and by all of us at Mother's Love. There was also great compassion amongst the Chinese population as they faced this surge of abandonment. This aspect is far less documented, but as you will read in the following chapters, many local Chinese people in the community wanted to and did respond. As a Chinese person myself, I hope that the adoptees reading this can relate to this spirit and be at peace with the Chinese part of their origins.

After years working for abandoned children and adoption in Hong Kong and in China, I am absolutely convinced that when they are ready, adoptees have the right to know. The choice to trace their history is theirs alone, and largely depends on their readiness to engage in this search. It may come early when they are young children, and in my experience, the sooner they start to establish relations with their past, the better. Or it may come later, when they are young adults. The physical journey today is limited in what one can see and experience of the past. This is, however, a positive change, as it shows that there is no longer a need for Mother's Love. In any case, for many adoptees this journey is still an immensely valuable experience.

In telling this story, I do not want to deny the reality of the horrendous situation where all this originated. The abandonment crisis of the early 1990s in China was a large-scale humanitarian disaster rooted in a combination of cultural, economic, and political factors, where the one-child policy launched by the Chinese authorities played a decisive role (See Appendix). This crisis created difficult and challenging situations, primarily for abandoned children, but also for adults as well. Like so many others, I personally had to confront the terrible reality in front of me, and despite the distance of time, it is still a shock to be reminded of those events. Some of the following pages are emotionally difficult to read, as are the facts they refer to. I do not recall them here for the purpose of darkening, blaming, or shaming. I include them because I believe the adoptees have the right to the truth. These facts are necessary to understand the despair and severity of the situation. They also highlight the initiative, commitment, and humanity of all those who together found the strength and resources to refuse fatality. Above all, these terrible conditions need to be acknowledged to fully understand the meaning and the value of each of these lives.

In the following pages, I want to share the story of what I saw when I first entered into the Nanning state orphanage and the small steps that I felt compelled to make that ultimately lead to the birth of Mother's Love. This institution was established for the sole purpose of empowering the local community to respond to the baby abandonment crisis—a national crisis of such magnitude that it immobilized many who wanted to respond but felt helpless. I didn't come to Nanning with this project in mind, and I often experienced discouragement, uncertainty, and helplessness along the way. It was a long journey, where every day, every step, and most of all, every encounter, mattered.

Me in Nanning, 1993.

The the title of the book, *Hidden Treasures*, is derived from the book of Matthew in the Bible, Chapter 13 Verse 44, included at the beginning of this chapter. It is the people from Nanning and how they generously loved me and their community that has been the greatest treasure on earth that I could have found. Indeed, many of them went through their own life-changing experiences and have discovered their own valuable treasures in the form of connection, meaning, and value— these individuals are inspirational to me. I arrived in China in my late 20s penniless, single, and with my family far away in Canada, and discovered a seemingly hopeless situation, one I simply couldn't turn away from. I felt incapable, alone, and burdened with an immense responsibility. I clung to the only thing I could travel with—my faith. Thirty years later, I look back and realize that I was about to discover the greatest treasure of my life. No amount of money could ever buy this joy.

The dream of writing the book first materialized in July 2014 during a conversation with adoptive parent Stephanie Balme in Hong Kong. When I shared my dream with her, she and her husband Richard matched my excitement and offered their book-writing experience to make this dream come true. We had often discussed the importance of returning to Nanning and to Mother's Love for their daughter Hannah and for their whole family. Richard took up the project and Jennifer Cheng, a journalist by training in her 20s, later on joined to help in researching and drafting the manuscript. Serrie Fung also brought her communications expertise to help edit and prepare the book for publishing. The four of us put our diverse skills together to conduct interviews, collect material, and draft and edit the chapters that now form this book.

As we aimed at giving voice to the actors of this story, we deliberately chose to start from memories collected in interviews, using an approach referred to as "oral history" in social sciences. Richard conducted long interviews with me (totalling some 15 hours of recording). Between 2014 to 2017, Richard, Jennifer, Serrie and I made a total of seven trips to Nanning to conduct interviews, take photos, and record videos. Over 30 interviews with retired government officials, former child care workers, foreign missionaries, adoptees and adoptive parents, and policy experts were made in Hong Kong, Nanning, and Beijing—23 of which have been recorded. The transcripts of these interviews formed the basis from which we drafted the chapters. We then revised and edited the text together until its final version. With the exception of Ms. Wu, whose name has been changed, we have used the real names of all the individuals represented in this book.

To give greater context to the situation across the country, we also collected statistical data from the Chinese government's records on population and reviewed the existing literature on the one-child policy, population, infant abandonment, and adoption in China. These details are included in the Appendix.

Finally, I also invited some of the adoptees and those whose lives were touched by Mother's Love, to give an account of their own stories, presented in chapter 6. In doing so, I hope that readers will see the legacy of Mother's Love living on in the stories of these young people.

Timeline

1970	China's population exceeds 800 million.
1979 – 1980	One-Child Policy launched in China.
1988	Kit Ying graduates from Guelph University with a Bachelor of Arts in Psychology and Sociology. She joins the Mother's Choice team, first as a volunteer, later as a paid staff.
1992	Kit Ying visits the Nanning state orphanage for the first time. She helps to facilitate the first two adoptions from Guangxi to the US in September that year.
1993	Kit Ying moves into the Nanning state orphanage, where she starts caring for babies in a shed on the orphanage premises and starts building a community of foster mothers. China freezes overseas adoptions for almost a year while it reviews adoption procedures across China. Channels for overseas adoptions are re-opened in November that year, with Holt International as the first international adoption agency to work with China.
1995	The Guangxi-Hong Kong Mother's Love Orphanage (桂港母亲之爱孤儿院) officially opens as the first joint venture between Hong Kong and China.
1996	Mother's Love begins training programs for child care workers across Guangxi and beyond.
1996	In collaboration with World Vision, Mother's Love launches pilot program to recruit nursing school graduates to work in orphanages in Guangxi.
2005	Mother's Love celebrates its 10th anniversary and begins to scale down its operations.
2011	Mother's Love completes its operations. Children with HIV are moved to a group home that would later become Radiant Hope.

1. From Hong Kong to Nanning: A Story of Southern China

I first became aware of the baby abandonment crisis and its reach in Guangxi province in 1990. At that time, I was working at Mother's Choice, a Hong Kong-based charity that serves pregnant teenagers and children without families, where I had been hired as the first social worker. I counseled pregnant teenagers and their families, and when we were short on manpower, I also looked after babies who were awaiting adoption in our Child Care Home. At Mother's Choice, I gained new perspectives from the diverse team that I worked with, I acquired new skills on how to care for vulnerable children, and I was exposed to new concepts like adoption and special needs—concepts I had had limited exposure to in my upbringing. At Mother's Choice, I absorbed these new experiences like a sponge, not realizing that they would set the stage for what would eventually become my lifelong vocation.

A Room of Silence

The early 1990s saw the peak of the baby girl abandonment crisis in China, largely a consequence of the sudden intensity in the enforcement of the one-child policy, combined with a cultural preference for sons (See Appendix). State orphanages were literally overwhelmed by the wave of abandoned baby girls. In Nanning, babies were found in all sorts of places—outside the train station, at the wet market, at the gate of the public hospital or of the state orphanage. They were found inside cardboard boxes or simply on the ground, wrapped with old clothes or newspapers. They were sometimes found with a small piece of red paper indicating the baby's birth date, other times with a milk bottle or with a few banknotes. Some showed signs of dehydration due to the hot weather and were surrounded by flies.

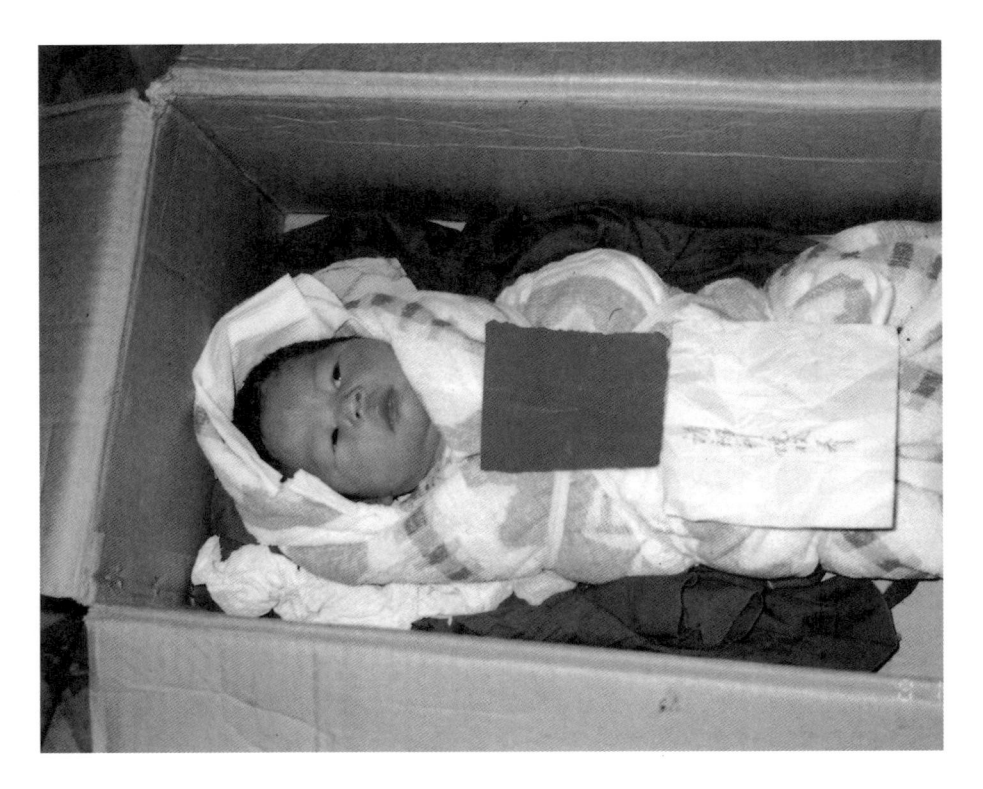

A baby left in a cardboard box with a slip of paper containing the baby's date of birth.

I first heard about the particularly alarming situation in Guangxi province in 1990 through some Western missionaries who traveled frequently to China. They told of the terrible conditions in the state orphanages. In 1992, I took a short trip to Nanning, Guangxi, China to assess the needs, with the intention of reporting back to my contacts in Hong Kong and to explore what help we could offer. This is how, without any formal introduction, I showed up one morning at the orphanage. The orphanage was the State Welfare Institution (南宁市综合福利院)—a residential compound where the elderly, mentally ill, disabled, and abandoned children lived together, as was common practice in China at the time. Armed with two bags of gifts for the children and staff, I went directly to the director's office to introduce myself and the purpose of my visit. The director seemed uninterested in my visit and without asking a single question, gave me permission to spend the day in the orphanage without supervision.

It was a blazing hot day. As I walked towards the orphanage, I could see a few children climbing on the metal gate. Seeing my approach, they opened the gate for me and greeted me as I entered the courtyard. A few of the children immediately grabbed my hand while others seemed indifferent to my presence. I was shocked at what I saw in the state orphanage, and what I saw that day has remained seared in my memory. Disabled children of all ages crawled around on the hot, rough, concrete ground. With the exception of a few teenaged girls, all of the children had short, cropped hair, making it difficult to identify their gender or age. They all wore tattered and mismatched clothes, some without pants. Some had rashes covering their faces, limbs, and scalps. Further in, there was a large room containing a few buckets for bathing and a single communal trench, which served as a toilet, shared by both males and females. Next to that was a room containing big buckets full of water and piles of clothes covering the wet floor—it was hard to tell whether the clothes had already been washed or not. Next to that were two rooms, each containing several children with blank faces sitting in a row of metal chairs with holes in the seats. These children all seemed to suffer from various kinds of disabilities. I later learned that these children were left sitting in exactly the same position in these 'potty chairs' from morning until night, when they would be returned to their beds. Presumably, these 'potty chairs' allowed the staff to save time from having to take them to the toilet during the day. As I walked around the courtyard, I could feel the children's eyes on me, begging to be picked up. I avoided their gaze—a part of me wanted to hold the children and play with them, but another part of me could see how dirty they were and was afraid of contracting any diseases.

I approached the baby room, which was in the far corner of the courtyard. Even from outside, I could smell the stench of excrement. Inside, I found three adult-sized beds with wooden boards in place of mattresses or bedsheets, with metal railings on the sides. Each bed contained at least 10 scrawny babies, lying side by side.

Disabled children sitting in 'potty chairs'.

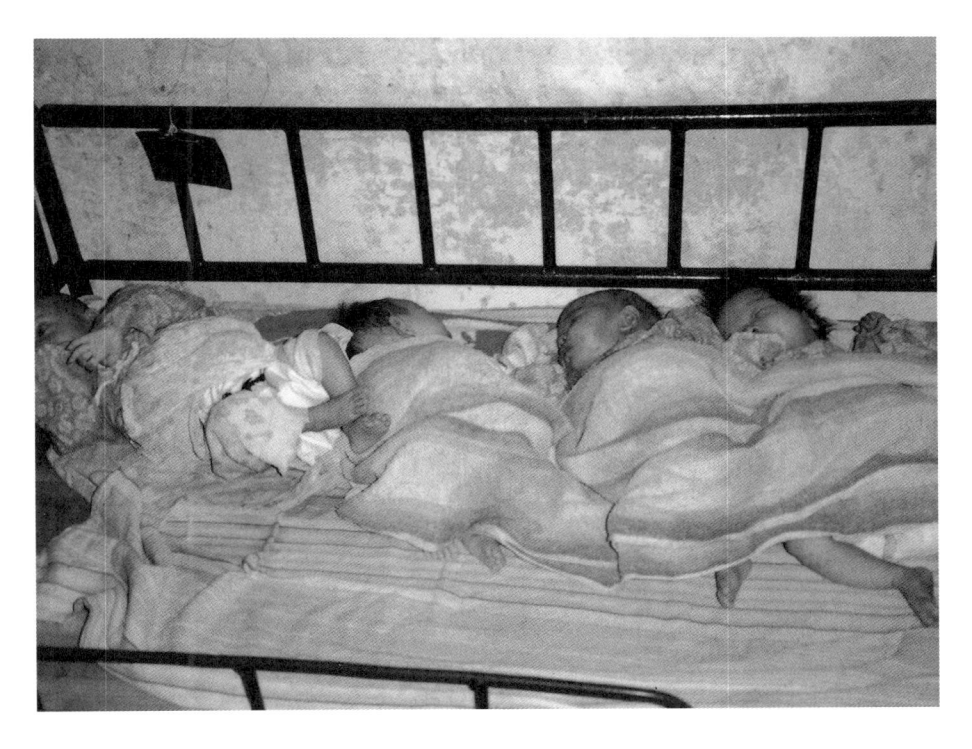

Babies lying side by side in the baby room.

The babies looked so emaciated that I couldn't believe my eyes. I had only seen babies so thin and frail in aid appeals for famine victims on TV. I walked over to the beds and looked closely at each of the babies. Their faces were gray in color. Their eyes were sunken in, and for the babies whose eyes were open, they had such blank stares that I couldn't tell whether they were still alive or not. Each breath seemed to take so much effort. Their "diapers" were made from old rags that were crudely fastened with string tied around their waists, and were loose and wet with excrement. It was eerily quiet for a room of around 30 babies. Suddenly, a cry broke the silence. I instinctively picked up the crying baby, who I later learned had been named Yuan Xia Hong (院夏洪) by the orphanage staff. I carried her outside to the courtyard where the older children were. After Xia Hong fell asleep in my arms, I returned her to the bed. As I turned around to look out into the courtyard, I felt dazed. I had never seen such suffering up close until that day.

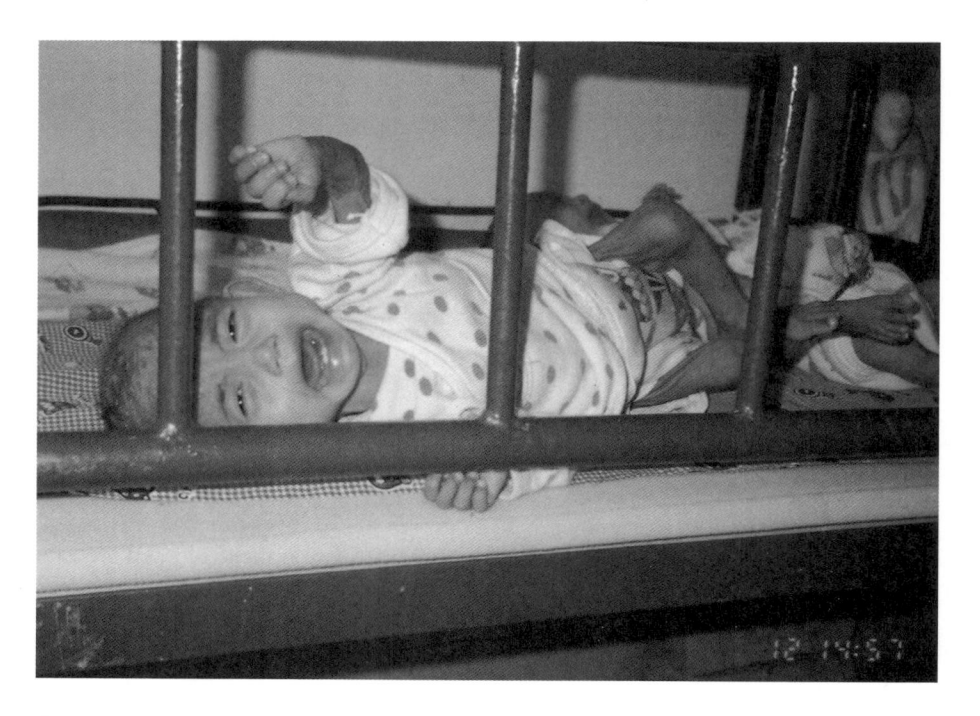

Babies left in the baby room.

As I walked through the compound, I realized that I hadn't seen a single *ayi* (a form of address for female caretakers such as nurses, cleaning ladies, child care workers, etc.; also an affectionate form of address for an older woman) attend to the hundred or so babies and children who were there. Later, I came to understand that the state orphanage operated much like a factory. Changing and feeding times followed a strict schedule, rather than being based on the needs of the children. Aside from those set times, the *ayis* were generally nowhere to be seen.

When I finally saw the *ayis* later, they were preparing what I thought was a big pot of milk for the babies. Upon closer look, I realized that it was thick in texture and that it looked like glue. It was in fact rice cereal, a thick porridge-like substance made from boiling rice in water, with very low nutritional value. Because there weren't enough *ayis* to feed each baby individually, these newborn babies would be laid out on their backs and have soft plastic bottles placed in or near their mouths. The tips of the nipples were cut off so that the babies could suck the rice cereal. Later, I would learn that the main cause behind many of the infant deaths in the state orphanages was rice cereal—babies were choking on the thick rice cereal that was fed to them lying down or starving to death because they were too weak to suck on the bottles.

As I was preparing to leave in the late afternoon, I returned to the baby room one more time. Xia Hong was crying again and I went over to pick her up. I couldn't bear the thought of leaving her there and I asked myself, "Why not take her back to the hotel with me tonight?" I carried Xia Hong to the director's office and told him, "This baby keeps crying. I would like to bring her to my hotel as I have one more day in Nanning. I will bring her back tomorrow." He replied, "Babies are troublesome. Why don't you take an older child?" I assured him that I was capable of looking after babies. The director didn't bother asking any details about my name, organization, or even where I was staying, and simply let me take Xia Hong. I later learned that outsiders were not permitted to take children out of the orphanage, but that day, the director seemed indifferent to my request and let me go with very few questions. I grabbed two items of baby clothing from the bags of gifts I had brought with me and set off away from the orphanage with Xia Hong in my arms.

I walked for 15 minutes in the intense heat down a series of narrow alleys before I reached the main road. As I walked, I looked down at this skinny, weak baby in my arms, and felt a flash of fear that she would die in my care. I quickly pushed the thought aside and hailed down a tricycle at the main road. I told the driver that I needed to buy milk formula and he took me to the only department store in the city, Nanning Department Store (百货大楼). The only bottle that I could find was a glass one with a bad nipple, but I bought it anyway, along with milk formula, which was very expensive at that time as it had to be imported. After returning to the hotel, I gave Xia Hong a warm bath, fed her some warm milk, and swaddled her in an orange hotel towel. As I watched her sleep soundly on the soft, clean bed, I knew that there was no way I could return her back to the orphanage.

Xia Hong and Xia Mei

Right away, I kicked into action. I called one of my contacts back in Hong Kong, a man named Mick Marshall, who had previously helped to facilitate intercountry adoption in China, and asked him to look in the pool of prospective adoptive parents to find a couple who could potentially become Xia Hong's new family. Looking at Xia Hong in front of me at the hotel, I knew I couldn't bring her back to the orphanage. She looked so peaceful—like a completely different baby from the one I had left the orphanage with just a few hours ago. I emphasized to Mick, "This is a very special baby and she deserves very special parents. Please hand pick the right family for her."

The next day, I visited a woman named Mary Fletcher,[1] whose contact I had received through Mick, in case I needed anything during my time in Nanning. Originally from New Zealand, Mary had moved to Nanning with her husband, who had a two-year contract teaching English at a local high school, and two sons. I visited her in her flat with Xia Hong in my arms. She gave us a warm welcome and exuded so much love and care that immediately put me at ease. I knew she understood exactly how I was feeling because she had been making weekly visits to the state orphanage for a while and she, too, had asked for permission to take home an infant and a three-year old from the orphanage, and was caring for them in her home. (Mary brought the two children home with the intention of "fostering" them, but later ended up adopting them.) We sat in her small living room and the emotions from the previous day came pouring out. It was the first time I had cried since arriving in Nanning. I was so relieved to be able to express my emotions, even though neither of us said a word. From that day onwards, Mary and her family became my main support and source of connection during the early few months of my time in Nanning.

That same day, I returned to the state orphanage and asked someone to come with me to the Ministry of Civil Affairs. I had previously helped a missionary organization to escort six families from the US to Fuzhou to adopt their babies in June that year. With my knowledge of the China Overseas Adoption Law and my recent experiences in Fuzhou, I knew that I could share this with the Ministry of Civil Affairs. The director agreed and asked one of his staff to accompany me. At the time, I didn't realize that I was fortunately in the right place to move things forward—the overseas adoption procedure could only be managed at the provincial level, and as the capital of Guangxi province, Nanning was exactly where I needed to reach a decision-maker.

---

1. Mary's story is highlighted in chapter 7 of *Love Has No Borders—True Stories of the Tragedy And Triumph Behind Intercountry Adoption*.

As we walked into the Department of Civil Affairs building, a grand-looking middle-aged woman welcomed us. She introduced herself as Ms. Wu. She invited us into her office and allowed me to explain to her why I was there. She listened attentively as I introduced my prior experience at Mother's Choice in Hong Kong, where I cared for babies waiting for adoption. I also shared my knowledge and previous experience with the China Overseas Adoption Law. She listened closely to my broken Putonghua, but her face remained impassive and I couldn't tell what she was thinking.

The next day, Ms. Wu called me at the hotel and invited me to her office again. This time, she not only asked me to share more about my intentions and my work in Hong Kong, she also seemed willing to move forward with Xia Hong's case. I gathered that she had visited the state orphanage and reviewed the China Overseas Adoption Law right after our meeting the previous day. Ms. Wu later became the main government official with whom I would partner to bring overseas adoption to Nanning and was instrumental in the birth of Mother's Love a few years later.

After a few more days in Nanning, I returned to Hong Kong for a few days to relay Xia Hong's information to her prospective adoptive family. Mary suggested that I place Xia Hong in the Nanning No. 1 People's Hospital (第一市人民医院) while I was in Hong Kong, knowing that she would receive the care she needed there. The hospital was near Mary's home and she knew the doctors and nurses very well, as her younger son had passed away from a tragic accident just a few months before, and had received treatment at the same hospital. Knowing that Xia Hong would be well-cared for in my absence, I returned to Hong Kong.

About a week later, on my second visit to the Nanning state orphanage, I was looking at the babies in the baby room when a cardboard box was brought into the room. Inside was a pink, healthy-looking baby with beautiful black hair, wrapped in a newspaper. Her umbilical cord was still attached, and she hadn't been bathed yet, so was covered with dried blood. She had very likely been born within the last 24 hours.

I picked up the baby and took her back to my hotel with permission from the director. I later learned that she had been named Yuan Xia Mei (院夏美) by the orphanage staff. She was the second baby that I had taken out of the orphanage within three weeks. Knowing that we had already identified adoptive parents for Xia Hong, I was confident we would find special parents for Xia Mei as well. Sure enough, when I called Mick Marshall and described this new baby girl, he told me that he had a couple already waiting to adopt. When I returned to Hong Kong again for a few days to pick up Xia Hong and Xia Mei's parents, I reached out to Xu Yiwei (徐意伟), a local interpreter for foreign teachers in Nanning who I knew through Mary Fletcher, and asked Xu's mother to look after Xia Mei while I was away. I returned to Nanning after a few days with two couples from the United States to adopt the two babies. In September 1992, these two little girls (later renamed Carissa Kit Ying Kono and Natalie Xia Mei Henes by their parents) became the first two babies to be legally adopted overseas from Guangxi province. Ms. Wu oversaw the entire process and this became her pilot for overseas adoption. Even though there was much confusion at that time between the split in roles and responsibilities between the Department of Justice and Department of Civil Affairs, Ms. Wu always managed to push through and continued to proactively collaborate with both departments to ensure things moved forward according to the law.

Xia Hong, later renamed Carissa Kit Ying Kono, meeting her adoptive parents for the first time in 1992.

Xia Mei, later renamed Natalie Xia Mei Henes, meeting her adoptive parents for the first time.

One Sunday afternoon during my second trip to Nanning, I felt a strong urge compelling me to go to the orphanage. As soon as the children saw me approaching, they opened the gate. I walked straight to one of the bedrooms, where a baby was lying on the wooden bed by herself. The baby had a high fever and was very dehydrated. She was covered in ants and flies. Without a second thought I picked her up and walked out of the orphanage, telling the *ayis* that I was taking her to the hospital. As this was only my second visit to Nanning, I had no idea where the closest hospital was, but I knew I had to keep walking if I wanted to save this baby's life. Walking under the hot sun with this sick baby in my arms, the narrow alleys seemed even longer than I remembered from my first day with Xia Hong. Out of nowhere, a motorcycle stopped right beside me and the driver told me to get on. "I need to go to the hospital," I told the driver, whose face was covered by a helmet. Without saying anything else, the motorcycle drove me right to the Mother & Baby Hospital (新阳路区妇幼) on the main road. After the visit to the hospital, I ran into one of the *ayis* from the state orphanage, Dawei *ayi* (大卫呀姨). Knowing I couldn't return the baby to the state orphanage, who was named Xia Yang (夏阳) by the orphanage staff, I asked Dawei to foster her. Surprisingly, Dawei agreed, and continued to care for her until Xia Yang was also adopted overseas.

That day stuck out to me—both my interaction with the mysterious Good Samaritan motorcycle driver who gave me a ride without a word about payment and whose identity I never learned, as well as my encounter with Dawei, who appeared just when I needed to find a home for Xia Yang. I am grateful for the presence of such "angels" who appeared in the right place at the right time when I needed it the most.

At that time, visitors to China were still kept under close supervision, and I was expected to report to the police station on every trip to Nanning to give a statement explaining the purpose of my visit. After a few visits, a female police officer asked to see me in her office. She asked me, "Why did you come to Nanning?" I immediately responded, "Have you ever been to the orphanage? Have you seen the children there?" And then I started to cry. I think that she was taken by surprise and totally unprepared to face such an emotional outburst from me. Instead of asking me more questions, she allowed me to leave. Later on, I bumped into her when she visited the orphanage. We simply smiled at each other. I don't know if she had come to investigate me or if she was visiting the children. All I know is that she never asked me any questions again and was helpful later on in issuing passports to the babies leaving China for overseas adoption.

Within three months, I had taken 14 babies out of the orphanage to help them to be adopted overseas. The hotel had become my baby room. The orphanage director approached me one day and said, "Ms. Chan, you spend so much of your time here now. Why don't you come and live here? It will save a lot of trouble going back and forth." I accepted without thinking, and it only sank in later that the director had been serious. The apartment where I was to stay was on the second floor of the building, past the first two blocks of the section for the elderly. It was the first door to the right. The director asked the maintenance worker to open the door and show me. It was empty inside and in good condition—a square-shaped single room of about 80 square feet with a window looking out to the outside corridor. At the back, there was a corridor leading to the bathroom and the kitchen. The director told the worker to reserve this room for me.

Growing Up in Hong Kong

In 1953, my father was the first from my family to migrate from Shantou, Guangdong province, to Hong Kong to join his uncles and cousins. After a year, my mother brought my older brother (aged 5 at the time) and my great-grandmother (in her 60s at the time) to join my father in Hong Kong, where he had managed to settle down with a job at my uncle's factory. Over the next few years, my older sister, two more older brothers, and I were born in Kowloon City, where my parents had rented their first room in a single story residential building. In following the Chan family business, my father later started his own garment factory, and my mother was a homemaker, occasionally helping my father in the factory. By the time I was born, my family's standard of living had already improved significantly. Even as a young child, I had the privilege of traveling on a plane with my mother to visit my father's relatives in Singapore. As the youngest daughter, I was loved and protected as *mei mei* (little sister) by everyone in my family. Growing up, I was always described by my mother as shy and timid. She expressed her love by being extra protective of my fair skin and doing whatever she could to keep me from tanning (fair skin being the standard of beauty in Chinese culture). My mother strongly believed that education offered an opportunity to change a person's destiny, and although my parents were not religious, my mother enrolled all of us in the Protestant schools in our neighborhood, believing that schools with Protestant or Catholic backgrounds would provide a strong foundation of values and excellent education to us, and later send us abroad for further education. Looking back, I believe my mother made the right decision in sending me to a school that ingrained in me the core values of 'Morality, Wisdom, Body, Unity, Beauty' (德、智、体、群、美), which laid the foundation for my development, and challenged me to ask big questions about the meaning of life—something that would continue into adulthood.

Growing up, I found that I had a natural connection to and an interest in babies and children. As a child, my favorite toy was a baby doll, and I would play with it for hours on end. When I was 12 years old, my eldest brother had a divorce. I was very affected by the difficulty of this situation. I was also very sensitive to and protective of my two-year-old nephew, who was caught in the middle of a custody battle. It was heartbreaking to see him put through such an ordeal, as I could see the trauma inflicted on him, but I didn't know what I could do. This was the first of many times that I felt the despair and sense of injustice in seeing a child experience trauma. This experience helped me to develop a sensitivity towards the needs of the children, and greatly influenced my decision to focus on child psychology and family studies at university.

At age 18, after finishing my Certificate of Education Examination (中学会考) at the end of secondary school, I followed my mother's wishes and went abroad to Toronto, where my two older brothers were living. From 1982 to 1987, I lived in Canada, completing my Grade 13 in Toronto and later attending the University of Guelph, majoring in Psychology & Sociology.

My Two Role Models

There are two important women in my life who have influenced me most to become who I am today. The first is my mother, who instilled in me a strong foundation of core values through her commitment, determination, and loving, nurturing character. The second is Helen Stephens, one of the four co-founders of Mother's Choice, who I met as a young adult, and who continues to nurture me through her great example of strong faith and guides me in my search for the true meaning of life.

My mother, although a petite woman with a gentle and kind nature, also demonstrated great determination and perseverance, and I learned much from her example. One of her greatest qualities was her generosity, and one incident stands out in particular in my memory. One day at school, an announcement was made over the loudspeakers, asking a classmate to go to the principal's office. I asked what the reason was, and I learned that her family had not paid tuition for several months. I went home and told my mother, who responded, "Then we need to help her pay her tuition," and proceeded to pay my classmate's tuition fees for the next few months. She carried a strong belief that education is essential to every child.

My mother also taught me how to relate to others, particularly showing respect to my elders, and expressing gratitude to those who had helped us. These lessons have been invaluable throughout my life, particularly during my time living in China, especially when I had to interact with government officials who were much older than me, and had no reason to listen to a young woman like me.

Me and my mother, 1967.

Helen Stephens is a beautiful woman with the most gracious heart, a strong faith, and whose love was expressed through action, not just words. As a child, I had only read about the lives of overseas missionaries in books, but here was Helen, a missionary in the flesh who had felt a calling from God to come to Hong Kong with her husband and children to serve the poor and the needy in the city. Helen saw me as a young woman, fresh out of university, looking for direction, and took me under her wing. Helen was always affirming and able to draw out the best in me. "Kit Ying, you are so easy to love," Helen would say to me. I learned volumes by watching Helen not only loved her family, but also those around her. Most importantly, I saw her unconditional love for the children who had no parents.

Mother's Choice

After five years of living abroad, I returned to Hong Kong in the summer of 1987 as a fresh graduate looking for opportunities to chase my passions. One day, I happened to see a local TV documentary,[2] which featured a newly opened home for pregnant teenagers called Mother's Choice. As soon as the program finished, I picked up the phone and called Mother's Choice to ask about volunteer opportunities. The home was run by a group of foreigners living in Hong Kong who saw a need for loving and non-judgmental support for young girls with nowhere else to turn to. To my surprise, I was not only warmly welcomed to the team, I was soon entrusted with the responsibility of accompanying teen girls on their hospital check-ups and visiting them when they delivered their babies. My two-month summer break passed by quickly, and when it came time to make a decision about my career and find my first job, I asked if Mother's Choice would hire me. Helen took a leap of faith in hiring me, even though they had no budget to do so.

I was hired as the first Chinese staff member. I settled in easily into my work caring for the pregnant teenagers and the babies who were living temporarily at Mother's Choice while they awaited adoption. I eagerly absorbed all of my new experiences at Mother's Choice like a sponge. I spent my working and personal time there, as I loved their ethos of living alongside the teen girls, their families, and the babies that they served. At Mother's Choice, I was exposed to the diversity of the team and

---

2.　"媽媽之家"—Hong Kong Connection 鏗鏘集 (1988)

supporters, who came from a variety of cultures and backgrounds, and met several different role models. In this new environment, I learned so much from each new person I met and each new culture I was exposed to, and my perspective broadened beyond what I had known growing up.

During this time, my innate maternal instincts and sensitivity towards the babies and pregnant girls flourished. My colleagues at Mother's Choice quickly noticed that I was good at caring for babies and children, and they would often bring me babies who were difficult to settle. This affirmation helped to build up my confidence that later gave me the courage to take risks.

It was also at Mother's Choice that I first learned about the concept of adoption, and the idea that you could love an adopted child as much as you could love a biological child. I remember the first time I handed over a child to the new adoptive parents. They looked at me through tearful eyes and told me how grateful they were for the gift of this child. I was floored by their comment—until that point, I had thought the babies were so lucky to be adopted, but in that moment, I understood that adoption is a two-way gift. It changed my perspective on adoption, so that when I called Mick Marshall from Nanning a few years later to find a family for Xia Hong, I didn't want him to find me just any set of parents, I wanted him to find me a special family, a family who would be a gift to Xia Hong as much as she would be a gift to them.

My Chinese Identity in Hong Kong pre-handover

My decision to move to China in February 1993 was the culmination of overcoming my own prejudices about the nation regarded as the "motherland" of Hong Kong. For a long time, mainland China had remained alien to me and I felt disconnected from this place. In 1989, people in Hong Kong reacted strongly to the June 4th Tiananmen Square Massacre, and took to the streets in rage and grief. I was 27 years old at the time. Naturally, I was opposed to the massacre, but as I observed people crying on the streets and in church, I realized that didn't feel the same emotional connection to this news as those around me. I was not interested in political affairs and the student movement in China. Although I was born and raised as a Chinese person in Hong Kong, I didn't feel a sense of belonging to China. When China first opened up in the 1980s, I remember my parents would often buy all sorts of things, such as rice cookers and fans, to be taken across the Shenzhen border and given to their relatives. I remember going on one of these visits with my mother and finding the whole experience so unpleasant, leaving me with the notion that people living in mainland China were both poor and greedy.

My perception of China changed in 1990, after I completed a missions training course in Hong Kong, followed by a month of traveling around China. I set off on this trip with an open mind and it helped me to see China through a new lens. When I returned to Hong Kong, I realized that I had once held such a critical opinion of China. I also began to sense a growing desire in my heart to return to China and do something there.

In 1992, Hong Kong was entering its last five years as a British colony and would be handed back to China on July 1st, 1997. A wave of fear swept through Hong Kong. People were afraid of what could happen after seeing what had happened during the Tiananmen Square Massacre. Many Hong Kong residents with financial means applied to emigrate to Canada, Australia, and the United States with the intention of living there and eventually obtaining a foreign passport. A foreign passport was considered the "get-out-of-jail card" in the event that China decided to close off Hong Kong under its sovereignty. This became one of the largest waves of mass emigration from Hong Kong that spanned from the late 1980s to the early 1990s.

When my parents received the approval notice to immigrate to Canada and join my second brother, I was faced with the dilemma of whether to join them or not. As the last remaining member of the family outside of Canada and a single person, I was eligible to join my parents. This was considered a golden opportunity by many, particularly during the few years leading up to 1997. I knew that I would have to stay in Canada for a minimum of four years before I would qualify for Canadian citizenship, but I could not forget what I had seen in the Nanning state orphanage and felt convicted to help the babies who were dying in the orphanage. I eventually decided to give up the chance to move to Canada, which so many other Hongkongers were desperately vying for, to get closer to the source of their fear, mainland China, to move into the Nanning state orphanage. I couldn't explain my seemingly irrational decision to others, but I knew that I wouldn't be happy moving to Canada, even if it was supposedly better for my future.

I returned to Hong Kong to celebrate Chinese New Year in January 1993. I spoke to my parents and each of my siblings individually to explain why I had decided to move to Nanning instead of joining them in Canada. They tried to gently persuade me to change my mind, saying, "Why don't you just move to Canada and become a citizen first. Then you'll have the security of being able to travel anywhere you like with a Canadian passport." Despite my family's efforts to dissuade me, I remained unshaken in my decision.

When my elder sister arrived in Canada, my family immediately sought the help of a lawyer, who miraculously secured a permit for me to enter Canada once a year to see my family. The permit was called the "returning permit", and I only needed to visit Canada once a year to retain the permit. It was truly a miracle that I was able to obtain this permit. I kept this until July 1997, when I decided to give up my permit, choosing instead to become a passport holder to the newly established Hong Kong Special Administrative Region of China.

In February 1993, I officially moved to Nanning, and Helen came to help me set up my apartment. Soon after my move, a newborn baby called Yuan Yu Fa (院雨发) and a seven-year-old girl with an arm deformity called Ming Er (明娥) came to join me while they waited for their adoptive parents. Every day, I would take Ming Er to school on my bicycle, then I would go to the market, return home to cook, and spend my spare time getting to know the elderly who lived in the same compound as me. My first few months of living in the Nanning state orphanage were my honeymoon period. Every day, I was radiant with joy and relished my time with the children, the neighborhood, and the community I was living in.

***

Even from a young age, I felt a deep desire to find my life's purpose. That first phone call that I made to Mother's Choice about volunteering opportunities marked the first step of many on my personal journey to pursue my calling. My experience at Mother's Choice expanded my mind and set me on a path that led me to the doors of the Nanning state orphanage, and later, a lifetime of work in serving vulnerable children.

Me, Helen Stephens, and Matthew Xu Yi Wei in Nanning, 1992.

2. Before Mother's Love

In spite of the baby girl abandonment crisis, I felt a tremendous connection with the city of Nanning from the moment I first arrived. The people were friendly and helpful—even the taxi driver at the airport welcomed me as if we already knew each other. From the beginning, the staff at the Nanning state orphanage accepted me into their community. Although people in the neighborhood looked at me with curiosity, they were always friendly, and often initiated conversation or made an effort to build a relationship with me. It was obvious to me that nothing would change unless people shared the same concern and care for these abandoned babies. However, as China had only recently opened up to the outside world, many people had never been exposed to any other perspectives and couldn't see a way out. The severity of the situation was simply too overwhelming for most people to know how to respond.

Xu Yi Wei, Matthew

On my first visit to Nanning, Mary Fletcher introduced me to Matthew Xu Yi Wei (徐意维), a Nanning local who was not only fluent in Mandarin, but also Cantonese or *bai hua* (白话), and English. At the time, he was an interpreter for foreign teachers at his college. Matthew worked at the Guangxi Financial College (广西经济学院)—the same work unit or *dan wei* (单位)[3] where both of his parents had taught at and belonged to. Matthew lived together with his wife and daughter in the same compound as his parents. Prior to my visit in 1992, he had been

---

3. A *dan wei* (work unit) is a place of employment in the PRC. It usually refers to large public or private corporations and public administrations placed under the supervision of a committee of the Chinese Communist Party. *Dan weis* play an important role in the implementation of the CPC's policy. They can grant authorizations for residency, access to housing or travel. During the maoist period they also granted authorization for marriage.

accompanying Dawn Gage,[4] an American English teacher at his college, on weekly visits to the Nanning state orphanage. He had also become a great support to Mary and Graham Fletcher when their younger son died unexpectedly in an accident. Matthew loved spending time with this group of foreigners. When I think of Matthew, I think of him riding his old bicycle, carrying his trusty camera with him.

Matthew was in his mid-30s when we met. Seeing the same scenes in the state orphanage week after week on his visits with Dawn Gage had made him feel hopeless. He shared, "It was hell on earth. The place just felt completely hopeless."[5] He recalled walking past an empty room in the orphanage where they had placed the babies' corpses, wrapped in plastic bags, waiting to be transported to the morgue. Inside the room, he once saw a bucket with a baby inside. "The baby was still alive, her eyes still open. It was as if no one even cared to save her anymore, because they were all going to die anyway." I could hear deep feelings of anger, sorrow, shame in my interactions with Matthew. In the face of these feelings, Matthew did the only thing he knew—he took meticulous photos of the children who came through the orphanage, capturing scenes from our daily lives in Nanning. Years later, these photos became like precious gold to us, because no one else had thought to capture these memories.

Growing up in Nanning in the 1950s-1970s, Matthew experienced both the impact of the Vietnam War happening just across the border and the consequences of the Cultural Revolution. These experiences left him fearful, insecure, and untrusting. Yet his mother's Christian faith and his interactions with the foreign teachers are his college challenged his thinking. Looking back on the hopeless situation in the state orphanage at the time, Matthew said to me, "Until you came, no one thought to take the babies out of the orphanage, because there was no help to be found outside. Even if someone took a baby out, it would still cost a lot of money and require a lot of resources to save the baby's life. Locals at the time held the mindset that even if you had that kind of money, it would be more worthwhile to use that money to save the healthier babies, who had a higher chance of surviving. This was an internal struggle for every Chinese person at the time—this question of whether

---

4.   In 1999, Dawn Gage founded Living Stones Village (http://www.livingstonesvillage. org/), a home for abandoned disabled children in Nanning.
5.   Interview with Xu Yi Wei, Matthew conducted by Jennifer Cheng in February 2017 in Nanning, China.

it was worth pouring resources into saving these severely ill babies. This is the difference in culture between China and the West. In the West, people will try hard to save someone who is severely disabled because they believe that every life is valuable. But in China, the thinking is that if you have the money and resources, why not spend it on saving ten lives rather than just one life?" He continued to express, "It is easy for all you foreigners to come to China to try and help the poor orphans in the orphanage. You can come and go as you like, but for us we have to stay here and continue facing the same situation every day."

Matthew's mother, Xu *ayi* (徐呀姨), was a wise woman with a kind and gentle heart. She was the first woman I asked to be a "foster mother", first caring for Xia Mei, and later with the support of Matthew's wife, fostering more than 10 babies that I took out from the state orphanage. At the time, Matthew's parents were both in their 60's, and found deep satisfaction in taking part in this adventure. To this day, I recall fondly Xu *ayi*'s delicious home-cooked meals. I was truly blessed by their generosity and hospitality throughout those years.

Ms. Wu

When I visited the Ministry of Civil Affairs for the very first time in August 1992, I went with a clear objective and a sense of urgency in my heart to make clear to whomever I met, that there was a solution, that there was a way out for such a desperate situation in the state orphanage. Despite Ms. Wu's proper and formal appearance, she welcomed me with openness. To my surprise, she listened patiently as I shared in broken Mandarin what I had seen in the state orphanage and my experiences with Mother's Choice and adoption in Fuzhou.

Recalling the early years of our relationship, Ms. Wu shared, "I was responsible for administering overseas marriages and overseas adoptions in the Ministry at that time. I remember the day I walked out of my office and saw someone who looked like a high school girl—you looked so young at that time. I remember that you came with Du Shuji (杜书记) (the party leader from Nanning state orphanage) without making an appointment. I had no idea what the orphanage conditions were like before I met you—I wasn't familiar with the operations of the orphanages as I didn't oversee that part of the bureau. At my level in the bureau, I was more involved with policy, funding, and some supervision. After hearing what you said in our first meeting and visiting the state orphanage to see the conditions for myself, a light bulb lit up in my mind about how we could introduce overseas adoption into Guangxi province. At the same time, in the back of my mind, I was always worried about the babies who stayed in the orphanage and whether they could survive. To be honest, no one knew how to meet the overwhelming needs of the abandoned babies at that time. Your arrival brought hope to these abandoned babies. I didn't believe there was a god, but I always saw you as an angel sent from above!"[6]

Although Ms. Wu and I are both ethnically-Chinese, we represent two different generations with two very different experiences growing up. I would never have thought that I would be able to persuade her to try adoption, a concept that was so foreign, especially since no one had ever done it before in Guangxi. And yet, I felt a deep connection to Ms. Wu that I couldn't explain. I was convinced that we shared the same concern about the crisis. Since then, Ms. Wu's drive and determination have made her a formidable advocate for abandoned babies and disabled children living in the orphanages in Guangxi.

In 1993, Mother's Choice invited Ms. Wu and her direct supervisor for a visit. This was a ground-breaking occasion, because these types of visits were not common at that time, and it was very difficult to gain permission to leave the mainland. After facing many obstacles, they were finally granted permission to visit Mother's Choice on April 20th, 1993. It was an eye-opening and reinvigorating experience for both of them. Ms. Wu shared, "I was very impressed by the facilities and the tidiness of the environment. I had never seen such a level of care given to babies and children. I was extremely moved when I saw how the carers loved and cared for the children with special needs. I had never seen children with special needs be treated with such dignity and something stirred inside me, knowing that the same group of children in China would have had to live in terrible conditions." I still remember that evening in 1993 when Ms. Wu approached me with tears in her eyes and said, "I have just realized there is still love in this world."

Ms. Wu played a critical role in bringing together the different parties in Guangxi and Beijing to make overseas adoption a reality. It was her ability to build partnerships that prompted her, after her trip to Hong Kong, to invite Mother's Choice to replicate their work in China by starting a children's home in Guangxi.

---

6. Interview with Ms. Wu conducted by Richard Balme on 12th December 2015 in Nanning, China.

Finding Community in Nanning

When I accepted the state orphanage director's invitation to live on the compound, I realized that I would be living in one of the blocks for the elderly. The elderly men or *gonggong* (公公) and elderly women or *popo* (婆婆) were delighted to have a young adult like me move into their community. "You are the youngest among us," one of them said with great joy. I felt very safe living among them, with my neighbors acting as my 'gatekeepers'. They would report to me the things they saw daily—who had come by while I was out, how many visitors I had. They were curious about my life and would sometimes even sneak a peek into my grocery bags, only to discover that I bought and ate the same food as they did.

I quickly immersed myself into the state orphanage work unit and felt very comfortable being around the *gonggong*, *popo*, and all the people who worked in the orphanage. They were intrigued about my motivations for moving to Nanning and wondered why a young woman from Hong Kong was living in the welfare home. I also adopted the local style of dress, wearing plastic flip flops everywhere I went. To get around, I either walked or rode a bicycle, just like everyone else. While they generally called me 'Ms. Chen' (陈小姐), I was soon given the nickname 'Miss Hong Kong' (香港小姐). I was open and had good chemistry with the people in my neighborhood, and they came to trust me. I came to love them and enjoyed being a part of the community.

I learned that many of the *ayis* were peasant women from rural areas near Nanning. They had minimal or no education. At the time, under the communist system, most individuals belonged to various work units. In those days, only a small minority of people chose to start or work for small businesses. Most of the *ayis* who worked in the orphanage had either been assigned there or found the job through personal connections or *guanxi* (关系). The social welfare work unit was considered one of the most unappealing and most lowly regarded in the hierarchy of work units in the government. It was a dirty job left to the least capable employees. This group of women of very low social status were tasked with caring for abandoned and disabled children who had already been disregarded by society. The longer I stayed there, the more I came to understand them. I progressively saw how impossible it would have been to demand the *ayis* to care for each baby with love and dignity while they had never been valued or treated with respect themselves.

Instead of being critical about their behavior, I came to empathize with them, recognizing that in such particularly demanding situations, we could not expect a person to give what he or she had never received or experienced before.

Still, individuals like Dawei *ayi*, who had helped me to care for Xia Yang, were true heroes in my eyes. I noticed that she often went into the "dying room" during her break times. The dying room was a room where the weakest babies, the ones who didn't even have the strength to suck on the thick rice cereal, and those who were critically ill were placed together. For these babies, their fate had already been decided for them. The thinking was that by separating those who had the slimmest chances of surviving, the staff could focus their efforts on saving the relatively healthier babies, but the fact was that all of the babies had a slim chance of surviving in the orphanage. Dawei *ayi* rescued a number of babies from the dying room and begged me to take them under my care. There was a toddler, Ai Lian (爱莲), who had a particularly special relationship with Dawei *ayi*. I found out later that she was one of the few survivors who had been rescued from the dying room by Dawei *ayi*. Ai Lian was later on also transferred to the care of Mother's Love.

Coming from Hong Kong, I found the mainlanders' mentality puzzling, especially in their approach towards caring for babies and children. For example, in the 1990s, the *ayis* fed the babies in the orphanage with a rice and water concoction called rice cereal. I learned afterwards that in addition to breastfeeding their babies, mothers typically also fed their babies another meal of rice cereal before bedtime. They believed that babies needed to supplement their milk intake with some form of rice, a more solid food, in order to keep them full throughout the night. On the other hand, alternatives such as milk formula were still served as a liquid, and therefore considered insufficient to keep babies full. Besides, milk formula was still a foreign concept in those days and was still much too expensive for most people.

Even though I knew that choking on rice cereal (due to it's porridge-like texture) was the main cause of death for many babies, I didn't want to jump in and intervene right away. I wanted to understand their reasons for feeding with rice cereal and I listened to their explanations of why they didn't believe that milk formula would be nutritious enough. I discovered that their approach came from their best intentions, based on their own experiences and cultural practices, and I felt ashamed of how I had quickly judged these women. Through modeling the use of milk formula, I slowly helped each of them to understand the danger of allowing a baby to suck rice cereal while lying flat on his/her back. Over time, the staff started to adopt the use of milk formula and stopped leaving babies to feed while lying down, not just in the Nanning state orphanage, but later in all orphanages throughout the province. It was most satisfying for the staff to witness the difference that they could make by changing their practices.

Although I moved to Nanning with the intention of helping the children at the orphanage, seeing their determination and resilience changed my life. I will never forget the day when I stood on the second floor looking down into the courtyard, and there I saw a few boys aged 5-10 playing together. Each of the boys was crippled in either one leg or both legs, and they were crawling or hopping around on the concrete ground, trying to shoot a deflated basketball into a big dumpster. As I watched, I could sense the seriousness of the competition balanced with fun and laughter. My heart swelled watching them play. I knew that these children had been abandoned at a young age because of their disabilities and were living in such conditions of deprivation, yet they were still able to find a 'way out' in their very limited circumstances in order not only to survive, but also to thrive. To this day, those children are still my heroes!

Out of the Orphanage into Homes

As soon as I moved into the orphanage, I knew it was of utmost importance to get as many babies out of the orphanage as quickly as possible. Babies kept arriving at the orphanage in growing numbers and they were dying every day. Getting them out of the orphanage was the only way to save their lives. I rode my bicycle around the neighborhood in search of women who would be willing to look after the babies for a modest stipend that came from Mother's Choice in Hong Kong.

A group of blind *ayis* who lived next to the orphanage agreed to care for the babies. They had been working for the paper-making factory (福利纸厂) work unit. Due to labor reforms and the industrial changes in the early 1990s, the factory had closed down, leaving many workers who were far from retirement age in the lurch. By the time I started looking for women to take in babies, many of them were looking for work. I still marvel at how seamlessly things fell into place—it seemed like the political and social situation were in our favor at the time. Some of the blind *ayis* had incredible stories of their own, and many of them had been orphaned as children themselves, and were intended to be sold as slaves. I was often told the story of how foreign missionaries had intervened in the nick of time and rescued them. Later, the missionaries started a school for the blind to educate them. For many of the *ayis*, they had not been blind at birth, but became blind from malnutrition in their childhood. Because of this, they understood the importance of proper care for the children and developed incredible skills to care for the children under their charge.

I approached these *ayis* and asked if they would be willing to take care of the babies from the orphanage. Ling *ayi* (陵阿姨), who was in her early 50s when I first met her, later recalled, "Ms. Chan asked me if I could look after a baby taken out of the orphanage. At the time, I had another opportunity to work as a masseuse. I decided to accept Ms. Chan's job offer because I could stay at home. However, I really didn't want to take the job. My worst fear was having a baby dying in my home. All the babies that Ms. Chan gave me to look after were all so ill."[7]

Foster moms, babies, and Christine Sams, a full-time overseas volunteer.

---

7.   Interview with Ling *ayi* conducted by Jennifer Cheng in February 2017 in Nanning, China.

Foster moms and babies.

News of this job opportunity spread by word of mouth and I eventually recruited around 40 to 50 *ayis* and I was excited about this small movement that was beginning. While each *ayi* received a small stipend from me (funded by Mother's Choice), it was clear to me that their motivation stemmed from their compassion after hearing about the need. It was work, but it also met a critical need in the community. The babies who came to their homes were usually ill and covered with rashes, and many of the *ayis* would spend more of their own money to buy additional Chinese herbs or food for the babies. There is no doubt in my mind that what the families gave to the babies far exceeded any money that I gave them. As I took the weakest babies out of the orphanage to put into the care of these *ayis*, none of them ever refused to take in a baby, no matter the challenge.

Ling *ayi* remembers how stressful it was to look after the babies because they were in such poor medical condition. "One had a wart in her anus which caused her severe trouble. I was very worried that the baby girl would die in my home. At the time, all the babies were girls. I remember their names. The first one was Mei Li (美丽). I took the baby to a Chinese doctor. She was able to recover without taking all the Chinese medicine. After two doses, she was already fine. I felt so happy seeing the babies getting fatter. I looked after Mei Li, my first baby for about 6 months. By the time Mei Li left, she was already able to walk. When it was time to bring the babies back to the orphanage, it was hard to say goodbye, but I would transfer my attention to the next baby, and I would feel better. After Mei Li, I accepted a second baby right away and this baby also had a rash from the poor hygiene standards in the orphanage. None of the babies stayed for longer than a year. I looked after eight babies in total. The one I could never forget was Chun Hua (春花). She was the fourth baby. She was a smart baby and she could walk at eight months."

I also liked to visit Ying Jie (英姐) who was also blind and had grown up in the state orphanage. When she became an adult, she joined the work unit for making cardboard boxes at the factory next to the orphanage, and that's when I met her. Although she didn't foster any babies, she still became one of my closest friends in Nanning. She lived on her own and was also a self-trained masseuse, and later even opened up her own massage parlor. "You're so tired, Ms. Chan. Let me give you a massage," she would often say to me. She would ask if she could practice her self-learned massage techniques on me, which I would gladly agree to.

Introducing Intercountry Adoption

In January 1993, the New York-based advocacy group Human Rights Watch produced the documentary The Dying Rooms,[8] which was aired on the British television channel BBC, exposing the horrific situation inside China's state orphanages to the world. The filming crew had masqueraded as representatives from an American charity visiting the Nanning state orphanage, taking advantage of the light security that had allowed foreigners to easily enter to help. The government responded to the exposé by banning all foreigners from visiting the state orphanages. I was not aware of the documentary at the time. All I knew was that foreigners were suddenly banned from the orphanages, but I didn't know why. I was surprised to see that no one was trying to kick me out of the orphanage. I remained living in the welfare home but without the

---

8.   The Dying Rooms is a 1995 television documentary film about Chinese state
      orphanages. It was directed by Kate Blewett and Brian Woods and produced by
      Lauderdale Productions.

usual stream of visitors, which left me feeling isolated and disconnected from the outside world. While I entertained thoughts of leaving, I knew I was already too invested in the state orphanage to move away. I had personally recruited all the *ayis* to foster the babies from the orphanage and I felt responsible for them.

Reports on illegal adoptions all over the country prompted the Chinese government to freeze overseas adoptions for several months in 1993 while new laws and policies were drafted.[9] The reality of what I had committed to in Nanning was starting to sink in. When I had first arrived, I would feel so excited at the sight of a new baby arriving at the orphanage that I would run to greet it. But by the summer of 1993, the honeymoon phase was wearing off. With the pathway to overseas adoption blocked, I soon began to feel trapped in the despair of the whole crisis. I had the feeling that there was nothing that could be done to alleviate the crisis, a feeling that many state orphanage staff had become familiar with over the years.

In my lowest moments, I would visit the blind *ayis* and watch how they overcame so many obstacles in caring for the babies. The blind *ayis*, having already raised their own children, were experienced mothers and kept the babies clean, properly fed, and very happy. Most of all, I enjoyed visiting Huo Wang *ayi* (活望呀姨), a foster mom who was willing to take on the most challenging babies including one with severe cerebral palsy. It was incredible to sit in her home and watch her prepare a meal. I watched her feed firewood into a stove and prepare an entire meal entirely by touch. When I saw how she didn't let her disability stand in the way of performing her daily tasks with ease, it somehow put my own discouragement into perspective and gave me the drive to continue. "What else do I have to complain about?" I would tell myself.

With the road to overseas adoption closed, I was also beginning to feel that I could not stand the terrible conditions of the baby room anymore. It had to be addressed somehow, but I knew it would be difficult to impose such a radical change on the staff. How could I model a different type of care and motivate them to change their behavior with the babies?

---

9. The period also corresponds to the preparation of the Hague Convention of May 29, 1993 on Protection of Children and Co-operation in Respect of Intercountry Adoption, the major international convention regulating intercountry adoption. China signed the Convention on November 30, 2000 and ratified it on September 16, 2005. The background of the convention certainly contributed to China revising its policy at the beginning of the 1990s.

I had the idea to create another room to look after the babies. I asked
the director whether he could give me another space to look after the
children. To my surprise, he offered me a shed on the orphanage premises
that the staff had been using to store firewood. I gladly accepted and
began caring for five or six babies at a time in the shed. I then hired
my first staff member, Ming Hong (明红), the daughter of the Ling *ayi*,
one of the blind foster moms. The orphanage staff would also come to
the shed after their shifts to help me.

Caring for babies in the shed at the state orphanage, 1993.

I was beginning to see small windows of opportunities in what had
previously seemed like a hopeless situation. Others in the community
also saw hope in what I was doing in the shed and came to recognize
me as someone who could offer an alternative path for these babies.
Chen *ayi* (陈阿姨), a woman who lived near the orphanage, had started
caring for an abandoned baby she had found. Many people, like Chen

ayi, took in babies that had been abandoned, but soon realized that it was unsustainable because the babies would not be able to obtain a residential permit or *hukou* (戶口), which in China gives a child the right to education and healthcare. The only way to obtain a *hukou* for the babies would be to bring them to the state orphanage.

Babies and ayis in the shed at the state orphanage.

When Chen *ayi* realized that she had to bring the baby to the state orphanage, she was reluctant because she knew that the chances of the baby surviving life in the state orphanage were slim to none. No matter how much people like Chen *ayi* wanted to care for these abandoned babies or even raise them as their own, there was no way to locally adopt them, and the potential consequences of taking them in were too high. When she heard about the babies I was caring for in the shed, she approached me, desperately asking me if I could take in the baby, and I gladly did.

Celebrating my birthday together with the babies and ayis outside the shed at the state orphanage, 1993.

Later on, Chen *ayi* became one of the women who helped to foster babies who had been taken out of the orphanage, and went on to care for more than 10 children. She was one of many women who came to me directly with the babies they found abandoned on the streets. Through fostering babies from the state orphanage (and later from Mother's Love), these women had a way to care for abandoned babies in their home, while ensuring the babies had proper rights to healthcare and education.

After China closed its overseas adoption channels, it became clear that a more formal process would be required. Through my connections at Mother's Choice, I brought representatives from Holt International,[10] an American adoption agency that Mother's Choice in Hong Kong

---

10. David Kim's autobiography *Who Will Answer* details the history of Holt International.

had partnered with, to Nanning in October 1993. With their previous experience and established track record in facilitating international adoptions of children from South Korea and Hong Kong, Holt was in a unique position to work in China. When China finally launched the Implementation Measures on the Adoption of Children by Foreigners on November 10th, 1993, and re-opened channels for overseas adoptions, Holt was the very first international adoption agency to work with China and the very first children adopted to the US were from Guangxi. In 1996, the Chinese government took further steps to ensure proper procedures were taken by launching a new department, the China Center for Adoption Affairs,[11] whose mandate included welfare of children in orphanages, domestic adoption, and intercountry adoption.

However, not everyone received this news with such optimism. The issues surrounding adoption are complex, and particularly within the Chinese context, the topic of international adoption provoked feelings of pain, shame, envy, and suspicion. In China, the dire situation in the orphanages was intricately linked to infant abandonment as a direct result of the one-child policy. The entire population had been impacted by this drastic policy, with many families having to undergo forced abortions or sterilizations. These unintended consequences of the policy caused massive suffering within the Chinese population, often on a very personal level, but it was also seen by some as a necessary sacrifice and hardship that had to be endured for the greater good. Many people felt a strong sense of patriotism and held the opinion that this was a domestic issue that could only be addressed by the Chinese themselves.

Although adoption meant removing babies from a terrible situation and giving them families, there was still a lot of opposition. Some accused me of being a baby trafficker (人贩子). Others would ask questions such as "What if the adopted children grow up not being able to speak Chinese?" or "What if they grow up not knowing how to use chopsticks?" I could sense that people were very worried that the babies adopted overseas would lose their Chinese heritage. Some people felt that letting these children leave China to grow up in a foreign country would be just as bad as staying.

Their criticisms made me question whether it really was the best option for these children to leave China and be adopted overseas. I understood that in an ideal situation, the children would be able to

---

11. This was in line with the recommendations of the 1993 Hague Convention.

stay in China and remain connected to their roots. Yet I also knew that even if the conditions in the state orphanages improved drastically, an institution is no place for a child to grow up in. All children deserve to be in safe, loving, and permanent families. However, the immense majority of families across China were struggling just to stay afloat, and local adoption simply wasn't an option. In the end, I knew that it was necessary to continue to help the babies be adopted by overseas families because China was simply not yet ready to look after the abandoned babies. Sending the children into overseas adoptive families meant that they would have the chance to grow up in a secure family environment and receive an education that they deserved. I also knew that no matter where the babies went, their Chinese identity was something that no one could ever take from them. I always believed that one day, they would want to relate to China, one way or another.

In 1993, I travelled to the US to visit Carissa and Natalie, the first two baby girls I had taken out of the state orphanage and helped to be adopted. I stayed with Carissa's family and was able to spend some time together with them. This trip was critical for me, because it affirmed my decision to pursue overseas adoption in Nanning. I saw how the girls were growing up in safe and stable families and I felt reassured that sending them to adoptive families was the right thing to do.[12]

Valuing Every Life with Dignity

Distressingly, despite all our efforts, many of the babies in the state orphanages could not be saved, and many, many lives were lost. The numbers were so great that the staff felt utterly helpless. Anyone would feel despair in the face of such a hopeless situation. Getting involved to help a single child was intensely emotionally stressful, especially when the outcomes were uncertain. Would the child survive even if we tried? What would be the point if there were still so many others? I could understand why so many people chose not to even try to help—doing so would mean confronting a seemingly hopeless reality.

Sometime on a winter day, the staff told me that a new baby had arrived who was particularly small and frail. She looked like she may have been born premature. I took the baby back to my apartment. It

---

12. To read more on Carissa's story, read Reader's Digest January 1998 article 'To Save a Child'.

was an especially cold day. The baby's skin felt cold to the touch, so I held her skin-to-skin that night, cuddling her under a thick blanket. She slept peacefully that night, only waking once in the middle of the night when she threw up some blood. That should have warned me to how severely ill she was, but at the time, I had no idea. I waited until the next morning before I asked an *ayi* to bring her to the hospital as I had an errand to run. Later that day, a staff member told me that the baby had died.

The news shook me. It was the first time a baby I had cared for had died. I felt as if I had given birth to the baby myself and I was facing the death of my own child. The baby's death was a reminder of the life or death work I was doing every day and it marked the end of my honeymoon period at the orphanage. While I grieved the loss, I felt that the baby's death also expanded my heart's capacity to love and the need to continue caring for these fragile lives. Although I was heartbroken about the loss of this precious life, I also knew that I had to go on.

On another occasion, I was told by a staff member at the state orphanage that a baby had just been dropped off at the entrance. After spending several months receiving abandoned babies, I was reluctant to run to pick up the baby right away, like I had done when I first arrived. I was afraid of what I would find, and waited until the other staff members took their lunch time siesta to go outside. At noon, I went outside together with Ming Er, the seven-year-old living with me. I found the baby by the rubbish dump. The baby was wrapped in clothes, but she was already dead, so no one had bothered to bring her into the orphanage. I instinctively picked up the baby girl to bring her inside to the baby room. Anything was better than leaving the baby's body next to a heap of rubbish. Ming Er asked me if the baby had gone to heaven. I was speechless and didn't know how to answer. Ming Er answered the question herself. The only thing I knew to do at the time was to make sure the baby's body was treated with dignity.

Every day, I kept count of the number of babies arriving at the orphanage. On one particular day, eight new babies were brought into the orphanage. The number, which had once excited me as an opportunity to rescue new lives, now only reminded me of the extent of the crisis.

It was common practice for state orphanages in China to give each of their children a common surname. For example, the Nanning state orphanage gave all of their children the last name of 'Yuan' (院), which means institution or orphanage. Children from Liuzhou state orphanage (also in Guangxi) have the last name 'Liu' (柳), which is derived from the name of the city, meaning willow. At the Nanning state orphanage, the second character of a child's name was derived from the season when the child arrived at the orphanage. For example, Xia Hong's name indicates that the child had arrived during the summer time (夏). While the orphanages gave names to every child, not every baby brought into the orphanage was registered—sometimes babies would arrive in the middle of the night and be brought straight into the baby room without ever being registered. It was especially heartbreaking for me when a baby died without ever being named or properly registered, without a proper record of her existence, however brief. I vowed that any baby under my care would be named and properly registered. It was important for me to ensure that even if a baby didn't survive, she wouldn't be forgotten.

* * *

Death was a common occurrence in the state orphanage in Nanning and elsewhere, and sadly in many cases, from entirely preventable causes. Most babies were born healthy, but exposed to infectious factors in the hours following their abandonment or when they arrived at the orphanage, where conditions were poor. The sad reality is that many babies passed away due to a combination of limited capacity of the state orphanages to cope with the vast numbers of babies being abandoned each day and a lack of education around basic child care. Feeding was a big problem because there simply weren't enough *ayis* to individually feed each baby, and the choice of feeding with rice cereal meant that babies often either starved to death because they were too weak to suck on the bottles or choked to death because of the rice cereal's thick glue-like consistency. Babies were vulnerable to germs in the orphanage through rashes and abrasions that resulted from lying on their backs all day or being left sitting in their bodily fluids. Most importantly, I saw how essential it was for the babies to be held and cuddled, but there were simply not enough *ayis* in the state orphanage to provide such care. I could see that this basic human interaction was absolutely critical to keep the babies alive. Understanding this would require a revolution within the orphanage.

3. The Birth of Mother's Love

After a couple of particularly intensive years of facing the life and death of babies in the Nanning state orphanage, I one day found myself standing in the courtyard of what would later become Mother's Love. As I looked at the 'mother and baby' statue that sat in the center of the courtyard, I could see the potential for many children and adult's lives to be transformed through this place. Even though this vision tugged at my heart, I found myself simultaneously battling the fear of being stuck in China for the long term, something which I had never intended to. I had to be clear why I was staying. I envisioned a place where Chinese people would take pride in themselves for taking responsibility to care for their own babies and children, where they would value each precious life and have the knowledge and skills to do so. This idea strengthened me to overcome my fear and hold fast to my commitment to stay.

An Invitation

By 1994, after two years of living in the state orphanage, I felt physically and emotionally exhausted, and I was ready to leave Nanning. I felt like I had done what I could for the babies by setting up a foster care program and helping to introduce international adoption, but there was still no end in sight. We were still overwhelmed with babies coming to the state orphanage every day and babies dying on a regular basis. Although the crisis had not diminished, I knew I had done my part, and I couldn't imagine what else I could give to the babies, even if I stayed any longer. I could leave Nanning with the knowledge that I had done my best, and that was enough.

At the end of 1994, Gary and Helen Stephens, two of the co-founders of Mother's Choice, visited Nanning. Visionaries as ever, they saw things differently. While I couldn't imagine a way out to the crisis, their experience with founding Mother's Choice enabled them to see potential amidst the tragedy in front of them. Their experience meant that they were uniquely positioned to respond to the need in Nanning. They suggested to me the idea of setting up an organization equivalent to Mother's Choice in Nanning to care for abandoned babies and to help them find families. As the idea formed, they asked Matthew, the interpreter, to show them available land in the area that could be potential sites for a children's home. On the last night of their visit, I sat in the Stephens' hotel room and listened as they continued to discuss this idea with excitement. In my heart, I dismissed their lofty idea. They were foreigners who had no idea what it was like to live and work in China on a daily basis, and what they were discussing was simply an impossible dream. I wanted nothing to do with their fantasies, especially since I was mentally preparing myself to leave Nanning.

A couple of days after the Stephens left Nanning, Ms. Wu invited me to her office. In this meeting, Ms. Wu told me how deeply moved she was by her visit to the Mother's Choice Child Care Home in the previous year. "I wonder, would it be possible for us to do something similar to Mother's Choice in Nanning?" Ms. Wu asked. My heart started pounding. The idea had come entirely from Ms. Wu—I had never mentioned anything along that vein before. Until that moment, I had dismissed the Stephens' idea as a fantasy, but hearing Ms. Wu, a local Chinese person, ponder the same question suddenly helped me to see the idea in a new light. Maybe the idea wasn't totally impossible after all, maybe there was hope.

I called Gary and told him about my conversation with Ms. Wu. As soon as he heard from me, Gary kicked into gear to start building support in Hong Kong for this idea. This was precisely the invitation he had been waiting for. Soon after our phone conversation, Gary returned to Nanning to begin the deliberations for Mother's Choice to start a home in Nanning.

This type of collaboration between a Chinese provincial government and an overseas charity (this was before the Hong Kong handover to the PRC in 1997) was unprecedented, so the Guangxi government solicited the advice of the central government in Beijing. The head of the Guangxi Ministry of Civil Affairs, Mr. Bai, was a kind-hearted leader who deeply loved the people of Guangxi and was acutely aware of the overwhelming crisis of abandoned babies in his province. He had previously visited Mother's Choice in Hong Kong, and visited the US with Holt International to meet some of the children who had been adopted from Nanning. In his consultation with the central government in Beijing, he willingly agreed to shoulder the responsibility in the collaboration with Mother's Choice, taking on the risk of doing something that no one else in China had done before. After much deliberation, the Guangxi Ministry of Civil Affairs decided that the organization would operate as a joint venture between the Guangxi provincial government and Mother's Choice in Hong Kong.

Choosing a physical location for the home was an adventure. We visited many strange and random places, including a chicken farm in the middle of nowhere. But one option stood out right away as the clear winner. This particular site was in the Cemetery of Martyrs, devoted to soldiers of the Sino-Vietnamese war of 1979. The building was intended as a rehabilitation home for army veterans, but it had never been put to use. The building was spacious and airy, with a courtyard in its center. Its design was perfectly suited for a children's home.

At the entrance of the building was a sculpture of a mother with a baby at her breast. Helen asked the officials for the name of the statue. Ms. Wu told her that it was called Mother's Love. Helen's jaw dropped in disbelief. Prior to the trip, Mother's Choice co-founder Ranjan Marwah had started discussions with other board members about the name of this new home in Nanning. They didn't want to use the name 'Mother's Choice'—they wanted to choose a name that would reflect the needs of the children we served. The name they had picked was 'Mother's Love'—China has historically used the word 'mother' to represent the nation, so the name felt particularly fitting.

Although everyone around me was busy planning for the birth of Mother's Love, I still felt stuck in Nanning. I felt too invested in the work to leave—I had personally recruited the women who were caring for the babies brought out of the orphanage (including a few *ayis* from the state orphanage and foster mothers in the community), and it was important for me to continue to personally maintain each of these relationships in the community. At the same time, I didn't want to stay indefinitely and there seemed to be no end in sight to the baby abandonment crisis. The thought of staying in Nanning for longer only filled me with dread—I couldn't see a future for myself. That night after the site visit, I sat in the hotel room with the Stephens and told them with conviction that I would not be a part of Mother's Love. I felt certain that I had given my best over the past three years and that my job was done. I had made up my mind to go to Canada to join my family. Gary and Helen listened in silence.

Mother's Love statue.

In my mind, there was a clear leader in line to head up Mother's Love. He was an American man working at Mother's Choice, overseeing the Child Care Home. He was married with children, which in my mind meant he was more stable and mature. In contrast, I was a single woman with no management experience. Growing up in colonial Hong Kong and working with missionaries from the West, I had subconsciously come to believe that only Westerners could be leaders. By all measures, I felt that he was easily the best candidate. Personally, I was terribly afraid of the sacrifices I would have to make if I were to take on this responsibility, and I simply didn't think I was capable. I didn't want this role.

Despite my reluctance, Helen and Gary approached me and emphatically encouraged me to take on the role of leading Mother's Love. "We believe in you," they told me. I cherished Helen and Gary's affirmation and their belief in me, but in my physical and emotional state at the time, the best answer that I could muster was, "I need some time."

Gary connected me to the University of the Nations[13]—a Christian university in Hawaii. In January 1995, I took a four-month leadership training course at the University under David and Carol Boyd, who later became my mentors. Carol Boyd[14] later became an expert in child development and would visit Mother's Love and Mother's Choice regularly to give training to child care staff. The four months I spent at the University gave me the psychological, emotional, and spiritual healing, and affirmation that I needed. It gave me time to reflect deeply on the experience I had accumulated during my time in Nanning, and re-ignited my drive to keep serving the children there. It also helped me to develop the planning, budgeting, and leadership skills I needed to bring a dream to life. Most significantly, the course also challenged my previous presumption that only Westerners were capable of being good leaders—a bias I didn't even know I had. My fellow students at the University of Nations came from all over the world, and as we learned together side by side, it finally sank in that all of us have the potential to lead, including myself, and it gave me the faith that I, too, could lead.

---

13. The University of the Nations (U of N) is a Christian university founded in 1978 with branches in 600 locations in 142 countries, providing programs in over 100 languages around the world. Its largest locations are in Kona, Hawaii (US), Jeju, South Korea, and Perth, Australia.

14. Carol Boyd wrote her doctoral thesis in 2013 on a study of factors contributing to or hindering the development of trust and functional family behavior (http://eprints.mdx.ac.uk/15774/).

Putting Ourselves Out of Business

I never set out to build a kingdom for myself. There was only one reason why I accepted the responsibility of leading Mother's Love. The objective was simple and clear from the very beginning—to put ourselves out of business. In other words, while we would continue to care for children in our home, our goal would be to train and empower the state orphanages in Guangxi province so that one day, they would be able to look after the weakest children themselves. This meant that the priority was to invest in the training and development of local child care workers. During my three years of living in the state orphanage, it bothered me that while locals and foreigners alike cared about the abandoned babies, there was a clear cultural difference in how they responded. Many foreigners thought nothing of simply stepping in and acting wherever they saw a need, but many locals felt helpless and couldn't see what they could do. I myself felt like I was straddling both cultures, and in some ways, much of my job at Mother's Love would be to help bridge the two sides.

Because of this, I knew that the major purpose of Mother's Love would be to serve as a training ground for local child care workers in Guangxi province. The heart behind Mother's Love was to empower locals to help the children in a way that brought dignity and value to both the workers and to the babies they cared for. We wanted Mother's Love to become a model for holistic care through residential and foster care services for the rest of Guangxi province and for its operations to be fully supported by local resources.

I wanted each of the staff at Mother's Love to know their worth. I wanted them to know that they were valuable as human beings and that they had a useful skill set as child care workers. If we wanted the babies to be loved with dignity, then we needed to start by treating the child care workers with the same dignity. Knowing their purpose and the difference they could make in the lives of babies would also help them feel valued as individuals.

During my three years of living at the orphanage, I spent a lot of time with the *ayis*. I learned that many of them came from the countryside and had to work in the cities to support their families. Many of them had received little or no school education and were illiterate. After a while, I also realized that many of these women had experienced abortions themselves because of the one-child policy. These women had already undergone such painful experiences, and were then given the enormous task of caring for an overwhelming number of sick and weak babies. Surrounded by the babies and the workers, one thing became clear in my mind: they were all orphans. It wasn't just the babies and children, the adults had been abandoned, too. Both the children and adults hungered desperately for love.

Preparing the Opening

In May 1995, I returned to Nanning as soon as the leadership course in Hawaii ended. Gary had completed all the paperwork for Mother's Love. A Western missionary couple who was there to support Mother's Love had already moved in. The organization was officially called the Guangxi-Hong Kong Mother's Love Orphanage (桂港母亲之爱孤儿院). I had personally recoiled from the word "orphanage"—to me, an orphanage was a place where children without parents grew up, but my intention for Mother's Love was always for children to stay temporarily while they awaited a forever family. Still, I accepted the name as it was necessary for the work to be recognized in China.

In preparation for the opening, we focused on hiring local personnel. Within three to four months, we had already recruited all 80 of our staff, to help with child care, administration, and the kitchen. We didn't even have to place recruitment ads in the newspaper. Women heard about the job opportunities at Mother's Love simply through word of mouth and came knocking on our doors. I also had a great team of overseas volunteers who had been connected to me through Mother's Choice, many of whom came with specific and relevant skills like nursing and education, like Cheng Yu Pei (郑于沛) or Pei as I came to know her, and Wu Mei Hui (吴美惠), who came from Taiwan and brought their respective expertise in nursing and education. Their invaluable expertise helped to shape Mother's Love into a truly holistic child care home and enabled us to meet the children's various developmental needs.

Many of the Chinese officials doubted whether I—in my early 30s—could really spearhead a home with so many babies and staff members. Nevertheless, in November 1995, the Chinese officials beamed with pride at the opening ceremony for Mother's Love—a home that was the first of its kind in the entire nation. Over a hundred guests from Hong Kong flew in to attend the ceremony. At the time of the official launch, we were already operational and had babies living with us. Guests were able to see the babies at the Mother's Love home and visit our foster homes in the community. In the evening, a banquet was held at the Majestic Hotel in Nanning.

The opening ceremony for Mother's Love, 1995.

The role of director of Mother's Love was assigned to a local government official, Ms. Liu. As I was not a local resident in mainland China, I could not hold this role. Instead, I represented Mother's Choice—the Hong Kong side of the joint venture—which would provide all the funding for Mother's Love. While I held no official title, I was recognized as the figurehead of the organization.

Before Ms. Liu was tapped to work as director of Mother's Love, she was an administrator at the Cemetery of Martyrs. This was an expansive park with colossal statues commemorating war sacrifices, particularly the Chinese military effort in the Sino-Vietnamese war of 1979, which took place near Guangxi province. The Cemetery of Martyrs where the Mother's Love building had been located was also administered by the Ministry of Civil Affairs. Prior to her appointment as director of Mother's Love, Ms. Liu had never worked in an orphanage or with children in any capacity. "I was not prepared at all and I was clueless about the operation of the state orphanage. I was personally not too fond of children so I was surprised that they asked me," she said.[15]

Ms. Liu's strengths were in administration and she put her skills to great use as director. One of her most important tasks was helping each new baby to transfer her *hukou* (residential permit) from the state orphanage to Mother's Love. This process was very important, because it gave each child an identity and sense of belonging in relation to their home at Mother's Love. "Everyone knew that this was a highly challenging procedure," said Ms. Liu. "Miraculously, no application was ever disputed, and the officials in charge of the transfer never really asked many questions." One of the most emotionally-taxing tasks that we had to do, which fell under Ms. Liu's responsibility, was choosing which babies from the state orphanage would be brought to Mother's Love. "On my first day, Ms. Chan asked me to go to the state orphanage to select five babies to be admitted to Mother's Love. The criteria for selecting the babies were simple and clear. We wanted to choose babies who were either the most severely ill or had most recently arrived at the orphanage." Ms. Liu explained that she had to apply these criteria strictly. "At the time, I didn't question why I was doing what I was doing, I just went ahead and did it. But in hindsight, I felt like there was a higher power helping me to along the way. Through the process of bringing the children from the state orphanage to Mother's Love, I was so personally moved. It was no longer a question of whether or not I loved the children. My whole life was fully invested. For every child that we carried out of the orphanage, we were giving her a chance at life."

More than 20 years later, Ms. Liu still recalls the emotional ordeal it took in taking a baby girl named Hua Lan (华兰) out of the orphanage. "It took me three attempts to bring her out of the orphanage. The first time I saw Hua Lan, her body was covered in scabies. Wherever I walked in the room, I could see her eyes fixed on me. She wasn't ill, she just had scabies, so she was far from being categorized as critically ill. I could only tell her, "Ayi will come pick you up next time." The second time I went to the orphanage, there were newer babies and babies who were more severely ill than Hua Lan. And again, I saw her eyes were fixed on me. I still couldn't bring her out. So I told her again, "Ayi will come pick you up next time." The third time I went to the orphanage,

---

15. Interview with Director Liu conducted by Richard Balme and Kit Ying Chan on 13th December 2015.

I couldn't pick her again. I was already stepping out the door when I looked back and saw her eyes fixed on me again. I felt awful, so I walked back and said, "I have to bring you out this time, because I already promised you twice." I was only supposed to bring five babies back from the orphanage, but that time I brought six little girls. When I returned to Mother's Love, I went to find Ms. Chan right away and told her that I couldn't bear not to bring the sixth baby with me. Throughout the years, I saw so many children who needed help, but we couldn't take all of them to Mother's Love. We were still hiring and training our child care workers. This was the balance that we needed to strike in thinking about how many children we could take in at Mother's Love." This is how the first babies came to Mother's Love from the Nanning state orphanage. We were all confronted with this terrible dilemma, this incredible moral burden of having to choose which children to bring out of the state orphanage.

Foster moms, children, and Director Liu in front of the Mother's Love statue, 1997.

Modeling Change

The scenes I had observed during my first visit to the Nanning state orphanage were grim, but I very quickly realized that these seemingly callous practices stemmed from a place of lack—lack of resources and lack of knowledge. The reality was that state orphanages were overwhelmed with the number of abandoned babies and there simply weren't enough child care workers to provide the individualized care needed for babies to thrive, and many of their methods prioritized efficiency over all else. For example, babies were changed and fed en masse according to a set schedule, rather than according to need. They often went for long periods without being bathed, and whatever baths they had consisted of a cursory wash in a bucket of water. Children with special needs were confined to "potty chairs" during the daytime, eliminating the need for child care workers to change and clean them multiple times a day. Babies were fed lying down, with bottles propped near their mouths for them to suck on their own.

When I started caring for a small group of babies in the shed, it quickly became clear that there was a difference in the condition of the babies who lived in the shed and those who lived in the main state orphanage. Although all of the babies started out in similar circumstances (the babies I brought to the shed were arguably "worse off" since I prioritized bringing the weakest/sickest babies to the shed), the babies who came to live in the shed showed a significant improvement, even after just a few days. The *ayis* who came to the shed after their shifts in the state orphanage to help me were curious about my work. They had little interest in child care theory, but obediently followed my instructions on how to clean, feed, and care for the babies. Although the *ayis* may not have been able to explain the reasoning behind these methods, they could see the the impact it had on the babies' health and disposition. More importantly, they could see that these improvements were the result of simple changes that were within their own abilities.

In the shed, we made sure that the babies were changed regularly and bathed on a daily basis. We didn't have the luxury of a bottle sterilizer, but we made do by boiling the bottles on the stovetop. We cuddled, talked to, and played with the babies throughout the day, giving them the stimulation and affection they needed. Milk formula was rarely used in China at the time (partly due to its relative high cost as it was mostly imported from abroad and partly due to a pervasive belief that babies needed something more "solid" in order to be full), but I knew that it was necessary in order for the babies to thrive.

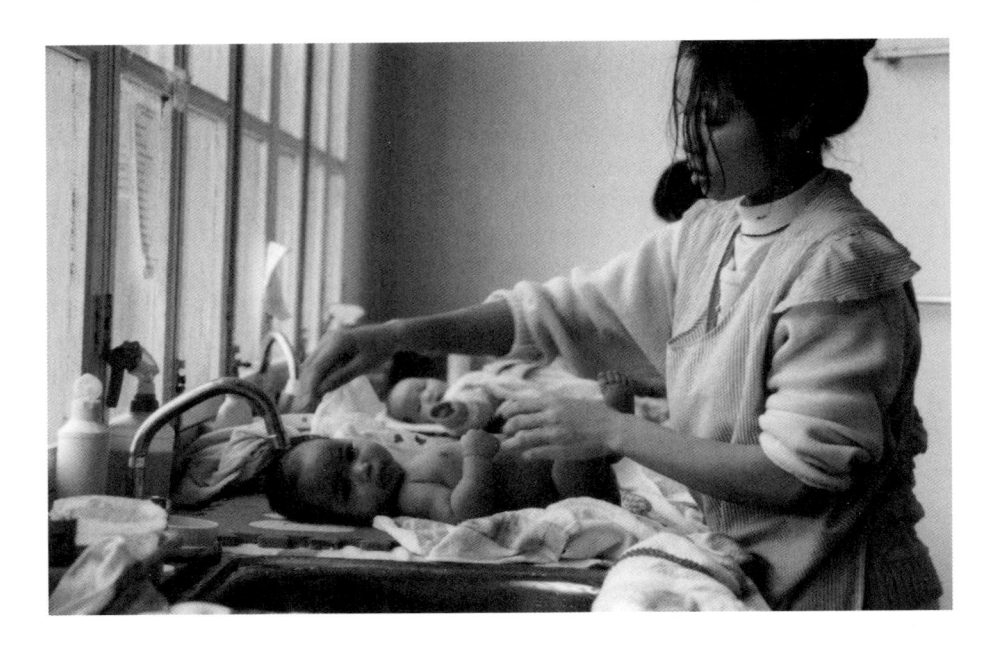

Child care workers bathing babies.

Later when Mother's Love began its operations, I was determined to use locally available resources as much as possible. I knew that if we really wanted to see a sustainable change in how babies and children were cared for in Nanning and beyond, it would be important to show the local people that they didn't have to rely on foreign aid to do it. Pei, the nurse from Taiwan, helped me to do thorough research to identify local options for things like good quality infant formula and baby bottles. For items that we couldn't source in China, such as baby bouncers, we found local craftsmen who could replicate the samples we brought from Hong Kong, using the materials available on hand. Once we found suitable sources for the items that we needed, we shared that information widely with other state orphanages. Over time, these recommendations were adopted as best practice standards for many state orphanages across Guangxi and even the rest of China.

Clean laundry hanging to dry in the backyard. The children's clothes and other linens were washed every day.

Transforming Child Care Practices

One year after Mother's Love opened its doors, we started running training programs for child care workers at the Nanning state orphanage. Soon, we were training child care workers all over Guangxi province. I learned that most workers at the state orphanages did not understand that babies could have feelings or have memories of their early childhood later on. They had never learned the importance of touch and human interaction to a child's early childhood development, and saw no need in holding and playing with the babies. The one-child policy reinforced ignorance and disregard towards pre- and post-natal child development.

The peak of Mother's Love training activity took place between 1996 and 2004. When we started training, we incorporated a lot of role play to help the child care workers develop empathy for the babies that they served by recreating the babies' experiences. For example, we would ask the workers to sit on a wet towel so that they could experience what it was like for the babies to lie in a wet diaper all day long. We would put the workers on the floor and feed them, and ask them to describe how they felt. This was an incredibly powerful activity for many of the child care workers, many of whom had never even considered the impact their actions had on the babies they cared for.

Me, playing with babies at Mother's Love.

In addition to direct invitations from state orphanages in Guangxi, other charities that worked in state orphanages from around China also invited us to train their staff, including Chinese Children Adoption International (CCAI), an American charity working in Hangzhou, and Christian Action, a Hong Kong charity working in Xining. In response, we continuously sent our staff to support these charities with training and support.

Word spread about the work of Mother's Love, and other state orphanages in Guangxi began sending their weakest babies to us, turning the home into a 24-hour emergency room. Up until 1998, the babies that Mother's Love received were usually critically ill, but many orphanages wouldn't take the babies to the hospital because the medical costs were simply too high. While we also had to pay for hospital visits, we fortunately befriended some medical staff at a nearby hospital who were able to take in babies directly into the paediatric ward—allowing the babies to receive medical care as quickly as possible.

Mother's Love staff member doing the daily task of folding piles of clean cloth diapers so babies could always have fresh diapers.

In 1996, Mother's Love launched a ground-breaking pilot program in collaboration with World Vision (an international humanitarian aid, development, and advocacy organization) where we recruited nursing school graduates to work in the orphanages. This was particularly significant because child care work was generally considered an inferior profession and not one that required any specialized skills or training. Our objective was to upgrade the child care sector in Guangxi province. If every child is valuable, then it only follows that the child care work profession is one to be respected. As a start, Mother's Love hired its first local nurses, Shao Qing (少清) and Yu Ling (玉玲). We went into the nursing school to recruit graduates to work in the state orphanage, explaining to the graduates that caring for the babies at the stage orphanage—most of whom required medical care—takes professional nursing skills. For the pilot program, World Vision subsidized the salaries of the nursing school graduates, the foster care program, and powdered milk formula at the Nanning state orphanage. We started off with a five-year contract and the goal was to transfer the funding for the wages over to the government over time. This process of transforming the child care practices of the workers took ten years. The pilot program was highly successful and later expanded to other state orphanages around Guangxi, and some of the nurses we initially hired from nursing school are still working at the Nanning state orphanage today.

**

In my first few years in Nanning, with support and funding from Mother's Choice, I focused on taking babies out of the state orphanage one at a time, nursing them back to health, and finding loving families for these precious baby girls. With the opening of Mother's Love, we continued to take babies out of the orphanages a few at a time, or we would receive referrals. We cared for up to 300 babies at a time—70 of them housed at Mother's Love, and the rest placed in foster homes in the neighborhood. We were able to scale our work—not by opening more orphanages or growing our home, but by modeling best practices and training child care workers from state orphanages throughout Guangxi and beyond. We established Mother's Love as a professional children's welfare home, with proper procedures and standards of care, and invited representatives from state orphanages and other charities to visit us and see what was possible. Through our training, we set out to equip child care workers with a strong foundation of knowledge and skills needed to provide an excellent quality of care to babies and children in their own orphanages. Through our partnership with World Vision, we pushed to transform the way the community viewed child care (and thus child care workers) by elevating child care as an important and serious profession. We knew that this way, we would be able to help more children than we would have been able to on our own.

4. Lives at Mother's Love

From death to life, from surviving to thriving, from abandonment to family, from the state orphanage to Mother's Love—we had come so far from the day I first arrived in Nanning.

Mother's Love became known across Guangxi province as the place where babies went for a last chance at life. It was a place where the caregivers loved each child as their own, and where miracles became common. Even though I had witnessed tremendous progress, the feeling of overwhelming needs and demands was still real. I was not any different from the rest of the Mother's Love team, but I realized that my early years of facing death in the state orphanage gave me strength to walk alongside them as they entered this challenging journey caring for these fragile lives.

Most of the time, I had no answer to their many questions about life and death, love, forgiveness, justice, and most of all, suffering. What I knew, however, was to show them that there was hope in the commitment to serve these children, and in the day-to-day interactions among the child care workers.

A Garden of Memories

Despite our best efforts, we were confronted with death on a daily basis, and this was a difficult reality that we had to face. During my three years at the state orphanage, I had seen too many undignified deaths of babies, and I knew we had to find a better way—one that brought dignity to each baby, and helped the staff process the grief that came with each passing.

In cases where the doctors had done everything they could, and it became clear that a baby was facing the final moments of her life, we would invite all available staff to join us at the hospital. Our staff would bathe the baby, dress her in clean clothes, and make her as comfortable as possible. Where possible, if there were no ongoing medical needs, we would ask the doctors to take the baby back to Mother's Love for these final moments. As a group, we would share memories of the precious life in front of us, and laugh and cry together. Even in death, I knew the power of human touch, and one of the staff would hold the baby (or her hands if she was too fragile to be carried) until she finally passed. This approach was so contrary to the typical practice in the state orphanage, and it was incredibly healing for me to see our team come together to value the life of each baby that came through Mother's Love. I could see that these simple steps helped the staff process the challenging emotions that came with caring for very vulnerable babies. It allowed them to continue to pour their love into the babies that lived without becoming overwhelmed by death. It allowed them to accept death without becoming indifferent. It was critical for us to value each baby as a full person and to remember her existence, even in death, no matter how fleeting her life had been.

In 2000, I visited the hospital after one of our precious children passed away. I watched a group of child care workers carefully clean and dress the child. It occurred to me how far we had come from the days in the state orphanage, where babies died without ever being given a name. I was so moved to see that this child had died with dignity and surrounded by love. As I stood there, an idea formed in my head for a place to preserve the memories of these babies.

This is how we came up with the idea of creating a memorial garden behind Mother's Love. We named this place the 'Little Garden' (小花园). I told my mother and elder sister in Hong Kong about the idea and they donated the crosses for the memorial garden. The morgues conducted group burnings of the deceased, so we weren't able to keep any of the ashes of the babies who had passed away, but when a baby died, we would hold a memorial service and place a small marble cross etched with the name of the child in the garden. The garden was a special place at Mother's Love for our staff to mourn and process their grief for the lives they cared for.[16]

---

16. As Mother's Love had to move out from its building in 2005, the memorial garden had to be removed from the place. The marble stones engraved with the names of children who passed away while under care at Mother's Love were carefully stored in wooden boxes. Their names are reproduced in the appendix as a tribute to all of them.

Memorial garden at Mother's Love.

Memorial grave for one of the babies.

Understanding the Pain of Birth Parents

Caring for so many abandoned babies, it was only natural to wonder at the reasons that would compel parents to abandon their children. Abandoning a baby is considered a criminal offense and severely punishable under the Chinese law. What then could push a parent to make such a difficult decision? These were the questions we faced in our everyday life at Mother's Love.

I personally never harbored any resentment towards the birth parents who left their babies on the streets—some still covered in afterbirth. In all the hopelessness and discouragement that I felt, I never once doubted that these parents cared deeply for their children, and that the act of abandoning their children was done in desperation when they felt they had no other option. Sometimes, parents would bring their babies to the doorstep of Mother's Love themselves. I would notice someone lingering outside the gate of Mother's Love, and on second look, they would have disappeared, leaving a box containing a baby at the gate. Normally, children at Mother's Love came from state orphanages where they first had to be registered. However, as we became more established, people started to bring their babies and children, the vast majority of them with special needs and some of them severely handicapped, directly to us. We accepted all of them. This is how abandonment came knocking at our door.

There is one set of parents who I will never forget. It was a Labor Day holiday, so our office was closed. The doorbell rang, and both Pei and I went to open the door to find a distressed-looking couple standing outside. The mother was very thin and sad, and was holding her baby wrapped in cloth. We invited them to come in and sit down. The mother gradually uncovered the baby and started telling us her story. We were shocked at what we saw. The baby boy was about five months old, with a head the size of a watermelon. His body was like a skeleton. His face looked gray and he was dehydrated. He didn't cry or open his eyes during the entire time his parents were at Mother's Love. The couple had come from a village in Bobai, a county far away from Nanning. They had come to Nanning to seek help for their son, but were told by the doctor at the hospital that there was no cure for their son, and that as he would die soon, it was better not to waste money on any treatments. The couple were under pressure from the father's parents to abandon the child, as they were uneducated about people with disabilities, and were afraid that he would bring bad luck to the family. The mother told us that she couldn't just leave their son on the street and she had begged the doctor to keep him. Instead, the doctor gave them the name and address of Mother's Love, where they came to beg us to keep their son. As our office was closed that day and we needed time to prepare ourselves, we gave the parents some money for lodging and asked them to return the next day. They returned to our doorstep early the next morning, and returned the exact amount of money back to us. As the mother handed her son to me, I assured her that we would do our very best to love and take care of him, despite the doctor's prognosis. I also wanted her to know that their son would be in good hands, and that even if he passed away, he would know that he had been so loved. Then she did something I will never forget. Right before she was ready to leave, she took the baby from my arms and nursed him one last time. Then she passed him back to me with a one yuan note from her pocket, and said that this was the only thing that she could give to her son. I was speechless and tried hard to control my tears. I could see that her breast milk had already stopped, and the one yuan note was probably all they had. Later we named him Adam.

Gary Stephens and Adam.

As I watched all of this, I saw for myself the despair and desperation that churned within a mother's decision to give up a child. In this hopeless situation, the parents simply couldn't see any other option but to leave their baby behind.

Embracing Children with Special Needs

In 1999, Mother's Love began receiving more and more children with severe disabilities and genetic disorders. Most of these children came to Mother's Love with cerebral palsy,[17] a few of them had hydrocephalus[18]. Although I asked Ms. Liu to avoid choosing older children with disabilities from the state orphanage, it turned out that many of the weak babies brought directly to Mother's Love were born with various deformities and genetic disorders that weren't immediately apparent.

As the number of babies with disabilities increased, I realized that those with severe disabilities would have little chance of being adopted and would likely require lifelong care. In my previous work at Mother's Choice, child care was only temporary until a child was adopted. I was not prepared for the possibility that the children would require long-term care. I wondered what would become of these children if they could not be adopted. I knew we couldn't return the children to the state orphanage, but I also wasn't sure whether we would have the capacity to continue caring for them. Personally, I also felt that choosing to provide long-term care for children with special needs would commit me even further, and on a more permanent basis, to Mother's Love and to Nanning, and I wondered how much more I could give. Confronting the growing needs of children with special needs also pushed me to think more deeply about the value of a life who would demand lifelong care and who might never be a "productive" human being.

Expanding our services to raise children with special needs in the long-term would also have implications on our resources—we would need additional financial support and would have to equip our staff with additional skills to care for children with special needs. I knew that I would need the support of Gary and the leadership of Mother's Choice

---

17. Cerebral palsy is a group of permanent movement disorders that appear in early childhood.
18. Hydrocephalus is a condition in which there is an accumulation of cerebrospinal fluid in the brain. Babies born with this condition suffer from an abnormally large head.

to support us. Gary and Ranjan shared my concerns—if these children required lifelong care, was I planning on staying in Nanning over the long-term to oversee this? I didn't have a solid answer, but I knew that we couldn't not respond to the needs in front of us. With their support, we created the 'Precious Group', which would focus specifically on caring for children with severe disabilities who demanded 24-hour care.

Precious Group special needs children with their ayis.

Soon, there was a growing number of children with various levels of special needs living at Mother's Love. Foster mothers in the community were willing to look after these babies while they were young, but once the children reached a certain age and became too demanding on the foster families, Mother's Love would have to take them back.

Pei with two of our special needs children.

When we took in Adam, the first baby with such severe special needs, he lived with Pei and Mei Hui, two of our full-time volunteers from Taiwan. We knew that the Mother's Love workers had never seen children who looked like this and if unprepared, they would be afraid of the child's appearance. Slowly, the three of us introduced him to our staff. Adam was met with curiosity but was soon embraced with the same love and compassion that they had showed to every other child.

China in the 1990s had little expertise or knowledge in caring for people with severe disabilities such as cerebral palsy or hydrocephalus. Pei, who had a nursing background, oversaw the medical care at Mother's Love and taught herself how to care for children with special needs by reading everything she could on the subject. I myself had a lot of questions about caring for children with special needs, because this was an area in which I didn't have any experience. I spent time at the Home of Loving Faithfulness, a home for severely disabled adults in Hong Kong, where I watched and served alongside the workers who cared patiently for adults with severe disabilities. Reading books by the

Catholic priest Henri Nouwen was also particularly inspiring to me. Nouwen himself had spent the last years of his life working and living at L'Arche Daybreak—a community home in Toronto, Canada for disabled adults. In Nouwen's words, "People with handicaps teach me that being is more important than doing, the heart is more important than the mind, and caring together is better than caring alone."[19] His words helped me to understand that each one of us is valuable, just as we are, and that our worth isn't dependent on our abilities.

As the children continued to grow, the need to provide special education became apparent. At that time, I also invited Mei Hui, who had previous experience in education, to start a special education class for the children at Mother's Love. Mei Hui spent nine years at Mother's Love from 1996 to 2004, when she returned to Taiwan to be with her family for two years, before re-joining Mother's Love again in 2006.

Jin Feng, Child Care Worker

One of the first child care workers invited to receive training as a special education teacher was Jin Feng (金凤), who had already been at Mother's Love for a decade. Jin Feng was only 18 when she first started working at Mother's Love. In total, she worked at Mother's Love for 16 years.

At the time, special education in China didn't exist, so the teachers had to learn as they worked. Jin Feng was responsible for teaching basic reading, writing, arithmetic, and life skills such as putting on shoes and cooking. Having cared for these children as a child care worker, Jin Feng already knew them well. As she recalls, "It was challenging to help children with special needs learn because their learning abilities were so low. Their disabilities varied. Some were deaf and mute and had a lot of trouble expressing themselves, but they could eat and put on clothes on their own. We had to repeat something over and over again until we saw some improvement. When we could see a student improve, the joy that we experienced as teachers was indescribable."[20]

In one life skills class, the teacher would take the children (aged 6-10) to the market to buy food, to learn how to prepare a meal from start to

---

19. Quote taken from Henri Nouwen's book *The Only Necessary Thing*. Crossroad Publishing Company, New York, 2008.
20. Interview with Jin Feng conducted by Jennifer Cheng on 5th February 2017 in Nanning, China.

finish. Because many of the children were unable to speak, they brought along paper and pen to write down what they wanted to buy in order to communicate with the shop owner. Afterwards, the children would return to school and learn how to prepare and cook the food they had bought.

When Mother's Love completed its operations in 2011, Jin Feng continued to work as a special education teacher at Silver Lining Foundation[21] in Nanning—a non-profit organization that helps children with cerebral palsy. "Before working at Mother's Love, I thought that a person was only valuable because of his or her abilities. If he or she was disabled, then what was the purpose of receiving an education if he or she would not be able to put it to use? At Mother's Love, what I really took to heart was that every individual has the right to enjoy a full life, and this includes education—no matter what they are capable of," she said.

Shao Qing, Nurse

Shao Qing was the head nurse at Mother's Love from 1997 to 2011. Prior to working at Mother's Love, she worked as a nurse in the public hospital, but left her job after giving birth to her son. After two years as a homemaker, her son began attending a nursery which gave her time to look for work. She heard that Mother's Love, which wasn't too far away from her home, was hiring, and decided to pay a visit.

She recalls her first impression upon walking into Mother's Love: "I was struck by how chaotic it was. The babies in the room were all crying. The staff were all running around. I didn't think I could work in such a place," she remembered thinking at the time.[22] We quickly offered Shao Qing a job working as a nurse. However, Shao Qing asked to work in the foster care department because she did not want to return to medical practice. "I had previously worked in the oncology ward at the hospital where I regularly faced patients dying from cancer. I didn't want to return to the medical field because I was afraid of facing death all the time."

After returning home that day, Shao Qing received a personal call

---

21. Silver Lining Foundation (雲彩行動) was founded in Nanning in 2007 to care for orphans with disabilities. The Silver Lining Rehabilitation Centre for children with cerebral palsy opened in 2011 in Nanning.
22. Interview with Shao Qing conducted by Richard Balme and Jennifer Cheng on 10th July 2016 in Nanning, China.

from a colleague at Mother's Love inviting her again to join the team as a nurse. She finally agreed to accept the job offer. "When I explored job opportunities at Mother's Love, I wasn't thinking about my career, I was simply looking for a job. I didn't expect to work there for long. Gradually, it was the children at Mother's Love who softened my heart. The longer I spent at Mother's Love, the more I realized that I was carrying the needs of the children in my heart. And more and more, I realized I was becoming attached to this work."

In the earliest days of working at Mother's Love, Shao Qing was overwhelmed by the wave of abandoned babies being brought into Mother's Love. "There was one particularly day when I was just so overwhelmed by what seemed like an endless flow of babies being brought into Mother's Love. I excused myself, went to my office, and just cried. I resented these parents for abandoning their own flesh and blood. These babies were so cute, how could these parents do such a thing? Later on, I learned from Kit Ying to put myself in the shoes of the parents and understand the anguish they must have gone through. I learned from her the value of empathy and forgiveness. This was all so new to me and led to so much personal growth."

Shao Qing remembers one of her toughest challenges was having to decide whether critically ill babies should continue to receive medical care at the hospital. "I had to decide whether we would spend a huge amount of money and expend the manpower to help a critically-ill baby survive. We would pay several thousand yuan to the hospital—enough to cover the costs of caring for several healthier babies. We didn't have to worry about fundraising, but I still struggled in paying so much money to the hospital. The nagging question in my heart was, what if the baby doesn't survive? It all came down to one question—is the life of this baby worth saving at all costs? The answer was always yes. I had to make decisions like this all the time."

Shao Qing spent a lot of time liaising with the hospital staff. "The hospital staff were not always supportive of our decisions to save the babies. Some of the hospital staff would discourage the Mother's Love workers from spending so much money on saving the weakest babies. The doctors would tell us that the baby would not survive anyway or that the baby would likely suffer side effects of the illness for the rest of her life. We often thought that the doctor was just trying to scare us, so we persisted and chose to believe that the babies would defy the doctor's expectations. And often, they would. We would see the child care workers returning to Mother's Love looking more and more optimistic with news of recovering babies. Many of the babies at the time suffered from pneumonia so they would struggle to breathe and cough up phlegm. Whenever the babies succeeded in coughing up phlegm, the child care workers would wrap the phlegm in tissue to bring it back to show us. To outsiders, this may seem unthinkably gross, but to us, it was pure relief to see the germs finally leaving the baby."

Over time, the hospital staff were moved by how the Mother's Love staff poured out their love on each baby day in and day out. We built up a strong rapport with the hospital staff, to the point where the hospital would admit babies directly into the paediatric ward, without us having to wait in the accident and emergency ward.

"One memory stands out in my mind," Shao Qing recalled. "One night, I brought a new nurse to the hospital to see a baby whose health was in critical condition. Although it was the end of the shift for the nurse on duty, she decided to stay behind. We knew that the baby would not have long to live. Together, we stayed by the child's side until she passed away at 2:00am. It was incredibly sad for all of us, and we didn't want to just leave her body behind for the hospital to handle it. One of our staff brought over some hot water and a towel to clean the baby's body, and we dressed her in a set of beautiful clothes. The hospital staff asked us if we wanted someone from the morgue to come pick up the body, but I suggested that we bring the baby to the morgue ourselves. Surprisingly, the others agreed."

Shao Qing worried that the other staff would be afraid of entering the morgue. "It turned out that they weren't afraid. It was the new nurse, Run Chun (润春), who held the baby as we walked to the morgue. We placed the baby down and watched her for a while. Before we left, we put shoes and a hat on the baby and wrapped her in a blanket. Outside, I realized we were missing Run Chun. I saw that she was still inside— she didn't want to leave the baby. I went over and embraced Run Chun and told her, "We've tried our best already. We can leave." When our babies passed away, they passed away with love and dignity. This was truly the essence of our work. No matter how long or short their lives were, we did our best to care for them. Even though many of the babies we cared for passed away, our hearts were at peace knowing that we had tried our best."

Ming Hong, Child Care Worker

Ming Hong was one of our first child care workers. I met her when she was only 21. Her mother, Ling *ayi*, was one of the blind foster mothers who had helped to care for babies from the state orphanage.

At the time, Ming Hong had just left a job working at a clothing factory and returned home to live with her mother. I invited her to work for me in the group home that I had started in the shed at the state orphanage. She agreed to the job offer only because there were no other options at the time. She was one of the first staff I hired and ended up working at Mother's Love for 12 years. In an interview with Ming Hong, she recalls, "I always knew I enjoyed being with children. Children simply followed me wherever I went, it was so natural."[23] The longer she worked with us, the more she sensed how different the atmosphere was at Mother's Love, compared to working in a factory. "It struck me that these were two different worlds in terms of how people related to each other. At Mother's Love, we saw each other as sisters. We could be genuine with each other, but not so in other workplaces. Elsewhere, it seemed like everyone wore a mask. At Mother's Love, it was all about teamwork and getting the task done. We didn't care about who did more work. At Mother's Love, we were all so comfortable with each other and we could talk about anything."

Among the workers at Mother's Love, Ming Hong had always found it especially hard to face the deaths of the babies. "I saw many babies pass away during my time at Mother's Love, many of whom I really got to know and really adored," she said. "One experience that left a deep impression was experiencing the first death of a baby I had cared for. The baby was in the hospital, where we took turns doing 12-hour shifts to stay with the baby. I stayed with the baby in the day time. However, this baby was severely ill with pneumonia and her lungs had already solidified. I wasn't there when she passed away in the hospital. I was heartbroken because I had thought that all the babies who came to Mother's Love had hopes of surviving. I returned to Mother's Love feeling absolutely devastated."

In the early 90s, many of the babies who had lived in the state orphanage suffered from pneumonia. Workers would have to pat their

---

23. Interview with Ming Hong conducted by Jennifer Cheng on 2nd February 2017 in Nanning, China.

backs regularly to help them cough up the phlegm in their throats and help them drink warm water. Ming Hong later recalled, "I blamed myself for not patting the baby's back enough. The doctor consoled me and explained that she was already so weak and that both of her lungs had already solidified. There was no chance of her surviving. Nevertheless, I still felt wracked with guilt that I didn't do more to help her survive. During this time, Ms. Chan came to speak to me one-on-one and explained to me that all lives are in God's hands. I was familiar with the idea of God, having read a picture book of God as a child, and I gradually learned to walk through my grief with God."

One of the most important experiences for Ming Hong was in 1996: "There was a baby with special needs called Fu Li (福丽). She was unpleasant to look at because of her deformity. She disliked having people touch her. It required so much patience and skill to care for her and most workers preferred to stay away from her. For some reason, she took a liking to me and so I cared for her most of the time although I still found her very challenging. Fu Li passed away around the same time as another baby. The news of the two babies dying devastated me. I went to bed that night and had an incredible dream. I heard angels singing the song, *This is the Day That the Lord Has Made* (这是耶和华所定的日子). When I woke up, I understood something. I understood that we can't predict when a life may end. Our lives are all determined by God. It gave me the strength to keep going."

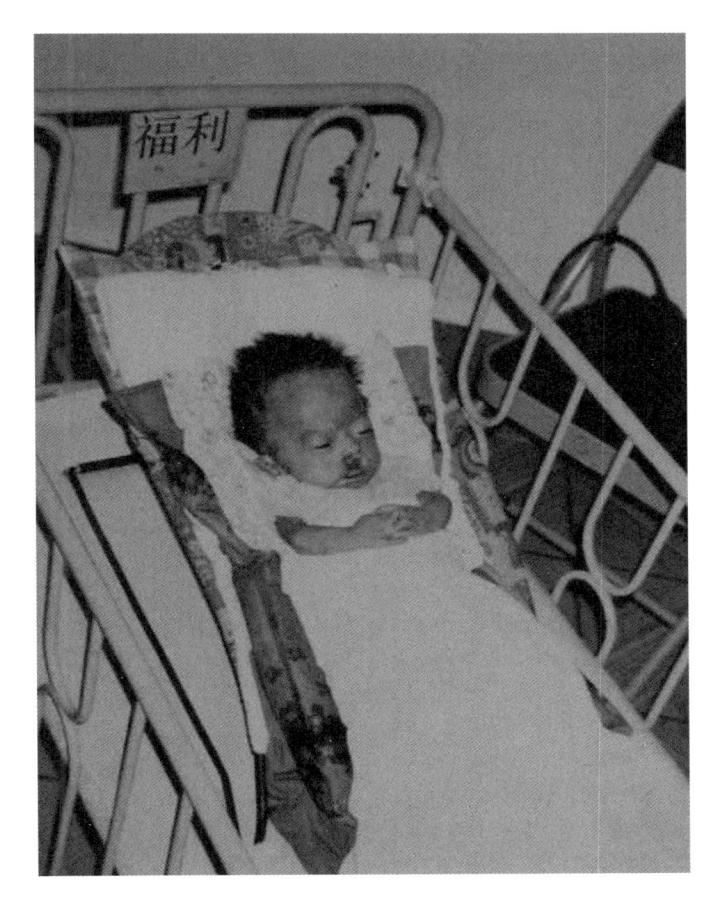

Baby Fu Li (福丽).

Hai Ping, Child Care Worker

Hai Ping (海萍) was also one of the first women I hired to work in the shed at the state orphanage. She was 31 years old at the time. She worked at Mother's Love until the organization completed its operations in 2011. In an interview conducted in 2017 in Nanning, she shared: "I was just looking for work at the time, when I met Ms. Chan who offered me a job. I had never cared for children before that. I had been working in a factory before meeting Ms. Chan. In the factory, people often used foul language and there was very little kindness. It felt so refreshing to be at Mother's Love. It was like my heart was cleansed. I felt so at peace there. At Mother's Love, I felt respected as an employee for the first time. Ms. Chan was stern and authoritative as a leader. At the time, many of us were intimidated authority figures, and Ms. Chan was no different. Nonetheless, we felt respected by Ms. Chan because she made the effort to ask for our opinions. For example, if she wanted to bring a child out of Mother's Love, she would first ask whether we thought it was appropriate to do so. I was more familiar with leaders who just went ahead and did whatever they wanted."[24]

Hai Ping recalled the internal struggles she faced in caring for children with cerebral palsy. She couldn't understand the purpose of exerting so much effort in caring for a child who would never be able function like an able-bodied person. "There were so many orphans. I wondered why we didn't take in more able-bodied children from the state orphanage? Even if the children with severe disabilities survived and grew up, what could they do? They needed lifelong care. Why were we wasting our efforts? Why didn't we focus on saving the able-bodied children who were dying in the state orphanage? These were tough questions that I didn't dare to ask openly. One time, Ms. Chan led a sharing session where she described how God had uniquely created each one of us and had given us these children so we could learn how to love. That day, I understood that these children had the right to survive and enjoy life like the rest of us. After hearing Miss Chan's sharing, it loosened the knot in my heart and it gave me a renewed strength to continue caring for these children with severe disabilities."

Shi Ping, Child Care Worker

Shi Ping (世平) was one of the first child care workers employed at Mother's Love. She was a young woman from the countryside for whom this was her first job. Her role was to accompany and care for the critically ill babies in the hospital.

In an interview conducted in 2017, she recalled, "I was so afraid when I first went to the hospital to care for the babies. They were so ill. I was so afraid of feeding the babies. I was at the hospital so often that the doctors and nurses all got to know me. In the pediatric ward, it struck

---

24. Interview with Hai Ping conducted by Jennifer Cheng on 4th February 2017 in Nanning, China.

me that most of the children had mothers and fathers, but the children that we cared for only had us. Sometimes in the ward, the parents in the ward would comment and say, "You guys have such a tough job." We would simply nod and smile."[25]

Being part of Mother's Love also led to a lot of healing for Shi Ping. "When I was 12 years old, my father passed away. I took on a lot of the responsibilities of helping my mother raise my younger siblings. I never really knew what it meant to be loved and grew up with a very low self-esteem. I envied others for having a mother and father who loved them. When I started working at Mother's Love, I could empathize with the babies on what it was like to feel alone in the world. I grew to really love the children and learned to stop pitying myself. Instead, my heart would feel so full around them."

***

When we think back to the lives that were touched at Mother's Love, we naturally think about the babies and children, but in reality, many of the staff encountered their own amazing life transformations as they chose to respond to the call to serve babies and children at Mother's Love. Many of them started with little knowledge or understanding about caring for vulnerable babies and children, but their time with Mother's Love pushed them to challenge their own beliefs and expand their hearts for the vulnerable. This journey brought them a sense of pride in their professional skills. At Mother's Love, they discovered the impact they could have on the lives they touched, the value of each individual life, and the knowledge that they could live in hope. This is something that each of them have taken into their lives beyond Mother's Love, whether they still work in the child welfare sector or not.

---

25. Interview with Shi-Ping conducted by Jennifer Cheng on 5th February 2017 in Nanning, China.

5. Bearing Fruits

In 2005, Mother's Love celebrated its 10th anniversary. It was a celebratory moment for all of us, but it also meant that it was time for us to re-evaluate what we had achieved over the past decade and to plan for the future. Our ultimate goal had been to 'put ourselves out of business', for the Chinese community to take responsibility for the welfare of its own children, and for there to no longer be a need for Mother's Love.

The Changing Landscape in Guangxi

By 2005, we had seen a significant drop in the abandonment of healthy baby girls. Not only were the rates of abandonment declining, we also received less referrals from state orphanages. Through the intensive training we provided, combined with our collaboration with World Vision to invest in the capacity of child care workers, the state orphanages had drastically improved their quality of child care, and many had even developed their own foster care programs and were able to work directly with the local government to facilitate international adoptions. In other words, the conditions inside the state orphanages in Guangxi and the death rate of babies had improved dramatically—a change to which Mother's Love had contributed significantly. By that time, it was increasingly rare to find able-bodied children inside the state orphanages. If there were able-bodied orphans, they would be swiftly adopted by families abroad.

Yet while the numbers of healthy babies being abandoned decreased, the numbers of babies and children with special needs continued to rise. It was clear that the needs in Guangxi had shifted, and that the most urgent challenge facing the state orphanages was caring for severely disabled children. I saw that if Mother's Love continued to operate, it would evolve to meet the needs of providing lifelong care for these severely disabled children, and we had to ask ourselves whether we were truly capable of going down this route. I knew clearly that this was not the goal that I had set out to fulfill when I decided to lead Mother's Love in 1994, nor did I have the experience, knowledge, and resources to do this.

With these changes in the child welfare sector, we decided to scale down our operations. At Mother's Love, there was only a small group of healthy babies in our care who were awaiting adoption, and we estimated that they would likely be gone within a year. We would commit to continue caring for the children with special needs, aged 3-15, in our Precious Group. With our reduced operations, I discharged a number of our child care workers. I explained the lessening needs and paid them each a severance. While the news about the lessening needs was positive, it was still an emotional moment for the staff. Many of them had grown to view Mother's Love as home and had become attached to their colleagues and to the children. Over the years, even though the wages at Mother's Love were not competitive and they could have easily found higher wages elsewhere, they had chosen to stay. For those who stayed, I focused on equipping them with the skills needed to care for the remaining children and their unique needs.

With less children under our care, we no longer needed as much space. We moved out from the main compound and into the apartments where I and other staff from overseas had lived. We remodeled the space to fit an office, kitchen and dining area, and rooms for the children, and continued to operate from those apartments over the next five years.

Finishing Well

By 2010, I could see that Mother's Love had completed its mission—to equip the local Chinese people to care for babies themselves. At the same time, a number of signs indicated to me that it was time to close Mother's Love.

In the 2000s, China rolled out policies that encouraged local social welfare organizations to register as charities, lessening the need for foreign charities. With the changes in the welfare and charitable sector in China, it was clear that the new needs would be better served by local organizations and its leaders. Separately, the Ministry of Civil Affairs informed us that the Mother's Love building would be demolished and a new rehabilitation center for army veterans would be built in its place (this was the original intention of the Mother's Love building when it had been built, but it had never been put to use until we moved in).

With both of these practical changes happening that would significantly impact the future of Mother's Love, I faced another tough decision. Should I continue to care for the 16 children aged 8-20 with medium to severe special needs, or was it time to conclude Mother's Love operations? And if we were to close down Mother's Love, who would care for these children? My answer came at the beginning of 2011, in the form of a visit from the director of the Nanning state orphanage. She met the children and observed how our child care workers cared for them. At the end of her visit, she expressed her desire to not only welcome the children to the state orphanage, but also to hire our child care workers. Most of the child care workers had been with the children for more than a decade, and knew the children's needs intimately. This was truly the best outcome we could have asked for—for both the children and the child care workers. Over the next few months, I worked closely with the staff to transition the children to the state orphanage.

In 2011, Mother's Love officially completed its operations. While I felt sad to see the children and staff that I had built such deep relationships with move on to the next chapter of their lives, I also knew deep in my heart that this ending was only possible because of the work that Mother's Love had accomplished over the years. I felt peace, knowing that I had played my part, and that completing our operations was proof of how far we had come.

Radiant Hope – Caring for Children with HIV/AIDS

While many of the older children with disabilities returned to live in the Nanning state orphanage, there was one group of children who could not move to the state orphanage—these were the children with HIV/AIDS. In 2007, Mother's Love had begun taking in children born with HIV/AIDS. It was extremely difficult to care for these children because of the siloed ways that services were provided in China. At Mother's Love, we partnered with the Ministry of Civil Affairs to serve abandoned babies, but serving children with HIV/AIDS fell outside of their scope, and instead fell under the responsibility of the Ministry of Health, which had its own set charities with which it could partner. A charity was unable to collaborate with both the Ministry of Civil Affairs and the Ministry of Health simultaneously.

That year, Pei and I attended a conference in Uganda that focused on the plight of children born with HIV/AIDS. I learned more about this emerging world issue at the conference and it inspired a conviction in me to help this group of children. Additionally, through our partnership with World Vision, we also learned of a growing number of people with HIV/AIDS in the countryside, many of them mothers and children. To prepare myself, I spent three months learning from one of World Vision's new projects in partnership with the Pingxiang People's hospital in the city of Pingxiang, about three hours away from Nanning. The goal of the project was to develop a hospice ward for patients with HIV/AIDS. During those three months, I encountered so many dying mothers who not only suffered great physical pain, but also the emotional pain of not knowing who would care for their children after they passed.

Since it was clear that Mother's Love would come to an end and that there was an increasingly urgent need of helping children with HIV/AIDS, I began looking for a successor who could establish a local charity dedicated to the care of the children with HIV/AIDS. The successor I had in mind was Ms. Wu, who had retired from civil service in 2009. She recalled, "At the time, I was 58 years old was spending some time in the United States visiting my daughter. In 2010, Kit Ying visited me and my daughter in the United States and shared about the needs of the children with HIV/AIDS. After her sharing, I asked myself, "What can I do?"[26]

In 2011, I asked Ms. Wu if she would lead a group home for the children with HIV/AIDS who were living at Mother's Love. She took a month to decide before accepting the invitation. "After my retirement, something in my life changed. I got to know myself in a new way. I found my purpose and I wanted to continue to serve children but in a new way," she said.

In the summer of 2011, I had found a building on the outskirts of Nanning that would house the office and the residential facilities for this new home. On July 27th, 2011, Ms. Wu began her role as director of this new home. The home started out with financial support from Mother's Choice, and became financially independent in 2016.

In 2012, the group home was officially registered as a local non-profit organization as Radiant Hope Child Development Centre (广西希望之光儿童社会工作中心). "People in the hospitals or state orphanages were clueless about how to help children with HIV/AIDS, so they

---

26. Interview with Ms. Wu conducted on 12th December 2015 by Richard Balme in Nanning, China.

referred them to Mother's Love," Ms. Wu recalled. "There was one other organization at the time which accepted referrals of children from the hospital or the state orphanage. However, Radiant Hope became the only organization that would take in children from the community without a referral."

The Spirit of Mother's Love

When Mother's Love completed its operations, many of the child care workers moved on to working for the Nanning state orphanage. The orphanage director at the time knew that Mother's Love staff were seasoned child care workers who were skilled and compassionate. The director apparently told the workers that he would hire anyone who had ever worked at Mother's Love. It was amazing to see how the spirit of Mother's Love continued to spread.

Many of the staff had spent a large portion of their lives working at Mother's Love. When they left, many realized how unique their working environment had been and strived to maintain the connections they had made there. Today, the former staff of Mother's Love continue to hold reunions every year. The women stay in contact during the year on a large group chat on their phones. The largest reunion takes place during Chinese New Year every year. In 2017, I joined them for a Chinese New Year meal, and was so moved to see how they had grown to embrace each other as family.

2017 reunion of Mother's Love staff.

Shao Qing and Yu Ling, Nurses

After Mother's Love closed, Shao Qing and Yu Ling, our two registered nurses, moved on to working at World Vision and began co-managing a program responsible for ensuring the quality of child care in Guangxi state orphanages.

Their leadership roles made full use of their rich experience in professional child care at Mother's Love (including Yu Ling's specialization in rehabilitation for children with severe disabilities) and allowed them to continue to influence the modernizing child care sector, where there had previously been very little expertise or knowledge.

Shao Qing and Yu Ling were also keen on bringing the same Mother's Love spirit to their workplace. "It's clear that our department is the most warm and tight-knit," Shao Qing says. "We would turn our chairs around and just start chatting. We organize fun gatherings outside of work hours that even people from other departments want to join."[27]

Liu Guang Xiang, Director of Mother's Love

Liu Guang Xiang's (刘广琪) life changed dramatically when she was asked to become the director of Mother's Love. She was a successful rank-and-file worker in the Ministry of Civil Affairs and had learned how to fulfil her responsibilities efficiently without getting emotionally invested. "I learned to complete my tasks but I would never do anything more than what I was asked. My attitude changed after I went to Mother's Love," Ms. Liu recalled.[28]

In 1996, the woman who oversaw our foster care services, a volunteer from Hong Kong, was planning to leave Nanning to return home. Ms. Liu asked me if she could take up the responsibility of overseeing foster care services so she could get to know the children better. "I explained to Kit Ying that I didn't know the children well. When I would give the baby to the adoptive parents, they would often ask me about the children, and I realized that I didn't know anything about the babies because my responsibilities were in administration," Ms. Liu admitted. "I felt quite incompetent because I couldn't answer people's questions.

27. Interview with Shao Qing conducted by Richard Balme and Jennifer Cheng on 10th July 2016 in Nanning, China.
28. Interview with Ms. Liu conducted by Richard Balme and Kit Ying Chan on 13th December 2015.

I was the children's guardian—the one sending them out of the country to be adopted, yet I barely knew anything about them. This hit me hard, personally."

I gave Ms. Liu the responsibility of supervising a hundred foster families and leading a team of four to five staff. Every day, she read reports of the children in foster families and followed their physical and emotional developments closely. She enjoyed the role thoroughly. In addition to her role as director, Ms. Liu also fostered a baby girl for a short period of time—taking the baby home with her every night, then bringing her back to Mother's Love when she came back for work. Through this experience, she gained a deeper and more personal understanding of the work we did.

After Mother's Love completed its operations, the government still referred returning adoptees to Ms. Liu's home so that she could tell them more about Mother's Love. Every time a former Mother's Love staff saw Ms. Liu, they would ask her if any of the adoptees had returned from overseas. "Whenever I hear about adoptees returning to visit, I ask the former staff if any of them are free to meet this returning adoptee," said Ms. Liu.

Ms. Liu is amazed by how the staff still remember clearly the children they care for and it is still the topic they talk about the most. "After all these years, the women still talk most excitedly about the children they cared for at Mother's Love. Today, it is still always about the children. They don't focus on talking about their current jobs. It doesn't matter if Mother's Love is not around physically—the spirit is still there."

At Mother's Love, Ms. Liu remembers most fondly the camaraderie among the women and their commitment to teamwork. At the time, many of the unmarried workers lived in the Mother's Love building because their homes were so far away. The babies would often need emergency assistance in the middle of the night, and she recalls the young women waking up right away to help. "This was the spirit of Mother's Love and it still continues to this day. Every time we have a reunion, these women all come back. Some of them started working at Mother's Love when they were only 17 or 18, and now they are mothers or even grandmothers. Every single one of them will look back and say their time of working in Mother's Love left a deep impression."

Ms. Liu says that all the workers recognize that it was the love they had experienced at Mother's Love that brought everyone together. She recalls, "In the past few years, one of the former foster mothers had some financial difficulties in her family. I asked the women over our instant messaging group for help and we began raising some money. Together, we raised around 5,000 yuan to help her out."

Shi Ping, Child Care Worker

Looking back on her time at Mother's Love, Shi Ping recalls how the environment was always very clean. She stresses how this was the basic principle embodying the dignity owed to the children by the profession. "Even though we didn't have a lot of space at Mother's Love, we made sure the whole environment was very clean. I think that came out of the love and respect we had for the children and for each other," she recalled. When Shi Ping and other child care workers moved on to work at the state orphanage, they brought with them the child care practices they had learned at Mother's Love, particularly best practices around hygiene and sanitation, to help elevate the standards at the state orphanage.

Hai Ping, Child Care Worker

Hai Ping, one of the first workers I hired, retired after Mother's Love completed its operations. Occasionally when the state orphanage was short on staff, Hai Ping would volunteer as a child care worker.

"What left the deepest impression during my time at Mother's Love was that I believed in Jesus. Believing in Jesus has been my greatest gift. I really believe God brought me to Mother's Love," said Hai Ping. "I used to be a very impatient person. After I received Jesus as my savior, something changed. Before, I didn't want to help anyone. Now, I really want to help others. I feel peace in my heart."[29]

She has been asked on many occasions to become a full-time staff at the Nanning state orphanage, but each time, she has declined. "I do not have to work for money," she said. "In the past, there was no way I would have been a volunteer. Nowadays, I don't think work has to be about money. Instead, I just love going to the orphanage and seeing the kids I used to care for at Mother's Love."

---

29. Interview with Hai Ping conducted by Jennifer Cheng on 4th February 2017 in Nanning, China.

***

In the early days at the state orphanage, I believed with my youthful naivety, that I was there to teach the *ayis* to love the babies and change the way they cared for them. But over time, as I got to know each of them and their stories, I began to see that many of them had personally experienced the impact of the crisis, and that they had been doing the best that they could for themselves and the babies. I saw each of them as beautiful individuals who were caring, friendly, and eager to learn new things. It's because of this that I knew Mother's Love would never be a permanent solution. I had full confidence that with the right support and resources, the Chinese people would be empowered to take full responsibility of responding to their own social needs.

6. Legacy

In 2011, Mother's Love as a physical entity and legal institution ceased to exist. The remaining 11 children under our care moved back into the state orphanage, entrusting their care to the local community that we knew were ready to take on this responsibility. Our staff dispersed—some of them following the children they had cared for by finding work in the state orphanage, some of them finding their calling in other professions. In spite of this, Mother's Love continues to live on today in the hearts of those whose lives were touched by this special place. It continues to live on in the continuing bonds between the children, staff, families, and community members.

In this final chapter, I want to share with you the stories, told in their own words, of some of these individuals who make up the very fabric of Mother's Love. Each of these individuals has a unique story to tell, but the thread that runs through their stories is that Mother's Love was the beginning of something—the beginning of a family, a calling, an identity. What they have gone on to make of this beginning to continue to impact the world around them is the true legacy of Mother's Love.

Carissa, Adoptee

"I am currently 25 years old and living in Seattle, Washington, USA. I am a lover of good food, travel, and exploration of new countries, and a good cup of coffee. After graduating from college several years ago with a degree in microbiology, I have had the opportunity to experience different careers and work in environments including working in a research laboratory and interning with non-profit organizations. Still wanting to do something in the medical field and wanting to work directly with patients, I recently decided to pursue the field of physical therapy. My life right now consists of working in a physical therapy clinic as an aide, volunteering in other areas of physical therapy, and going to school to finish up some prerequisites I need before applying to Doctor of Physical Therapy graduate programs.

I am the oldest child in my family and have one younger sister (not adopted). As we have gotten older and matured past the point of fighting every day, we have been able to maintain a close relationship and are a huge part of each other's lives. My dad is Japanese from Seattle and my mom is Chinese from Hawaii, so I actually look very similar to everyone in my family. So much so that most people usually assume that everyone in my family is biologically related. I wouldn't say that my family closely follows Asian traditions/culture, but small pieces of it have remained and it has been interesting to grow up with both the eastern and western influences shaping my life and values. Furthermore, having been back to China three times since being adopted and learning more about Chinese culture has definitely given me a greater appreciation for it.

I have been able to visit the city I'm from in Guangxi, once when I was 12, and again when I was 23. Both times, it was helpful for me to see places that played a significant role in my first few months. It was also interesting for me to picture what my life could have been like if I had grown up in Nanning—like what foods I might have eaten, the park where I may have gone, the apartment I may have lived in. Walking the streets of Nanning, I had this weird feeling like I belonged there—the city felt significant and part of my history. At the same time, I felt like I didn't completely belong there, maybe because of language and cultural differences, or because it was just so different from anything I'd ever known. However, it is still an important piece of my life. It's where I was born and a place where my life changed drastically, regardless of whether I was aware of what was happening or not. When I think of this place, it's with mixed emotions, but I like that I now have the real, hands-on experience of walking the streets, eating the specialties of the city, and being immersed in the smells and sounds myself.

Growing up, I struggled with the idea that my birth parents abandoned me because I wasn't good enough, because I wasn't the right gender, because the timing wasn't right, because of societal pressure, because of all of these things that I wasn't wanted. My birth mother, the woman who grew and carried me in her body for nine months, is supposed to be the one person in the world to love me, even if no one else does. Because of this, I struggled with the thought that there must be something inherently wrong with me for my birth mother to let me go from her life. A lot of my life I was angry and disappointed with my birth parents because of the choices they made about me. It wasn't until I visited Kit Ying a few years ago when I finally began to see things from their perspective, that maybe they did love me, but for one reason or another, life's circumstances prevented them from keeping me, their child. Maybe the choices they made were what they perceived as their child's best interests.

Me and Carissa in Nanning, 2015.

Throughout my life, I have struggled with trusting people. It has taken me a long time to realize that even if a relationship isn't perfect, and no relationship ever is, it can still have a positive impact on my life. I think I've tended to end or distance relationships before the other person has a chance to hurt me. I don't know how much of my past has influenced my struggles with trusting others, or if it's just my very cautious personality. I can say that my faith and family have been a constant source of love and support throughout my life. Knowing that I am a daughter of God and that I am pursued with love no matter what happened in the past has been such a source of hope, trust, and joy in my life.

Something that I was extremely blessed with growing up and even to this day is my family. I cannot imagine being placed in a more loving and supportive family. Yes, we have our fights and disagreements, but at the end of the day, we love each other. Furthermore, I am blessed to have been embraced by not just my immediate family, but also my extended family. One particular memory I have from when I was a lot younger was when we were on a vacation with my extended family and I was walking with my aunt and uncle. My aunt told me how happy they were that I was part of their family, and how excited their family was when they got the call that my parents were adopting me. I remember that it was the first time someone (other than my parents) had told me that they were glad I was adopted and had become part of their life. Even though that was years ago, it's a memory that has stuck with me and something that means as much to me now as it did at the time. As a child who often felt a little different from my other friends, none of whom were adopted, my aunt's words helped to give me a sense of worth and belonging into the life I was a part of.

Keeping a connection with Mother's Love is important to me because it is something that is significant to my story and something that makes my story unique. My life is where it is today because of Kit Ying and her faith and bravery, and that is a part of my story I never want to forget. Before visiting Mother's Love, I was interested in seeing in person where I was from, where my life began, but I was also interested in learning more about my story. My family kept a lot of the specific details surrounding my story from me, probably in an effort to protect me. However, as a 23 year old, I wanted to know the whole story, even the ugly details. Being able to spend a few weeks with Kit Ying and go back to Guangxi province was a great opportunity to learn more of my story and also really appreciate everything she's done both in China and Hong Kong. I think that going back to China when I was 23 was much more meaningful than when I first went when I was 12 years old. At that young age, the trip was fun, the sites were mesmerizing, and the food was good, but at 23 it became a lot more personal and I was able to process my thoughts and emotions at a much deeper level. It was deeper than just getting out of a van and taking a picture in front of something my parents had seen when they picked me up as a baby. At an older age, I was struck by the gravity of the situation and what happened, but I was also able to see redemption and restoration in my own life. Being part of a story that was once unwanted, abandoned, and broken and watching it be transformed into something beautiful is to me a picture of the grace and love of Jesus at its finest.

What I really came away with from this experience was peace— peace that even with all the unknowns I have about my early life and all the brokenness of those events, it's all right. I may never have the answers to my every question, and that's okay. It challenged me to look around at my life and be thankful for all that I have been blessed with – adoption, family, friends, and so much more—and be so very thankful for the gift of adoption and the voice and story that I get to pass on to others through it.

At this point in my life, I am pretty sure I know all that I can ever know about how my life started. While I would be interested in connecting with my birth parents, at this point it seems like a near impossible task. I would so love, though, to be able to see them in person, to learn if they had any other children before or after me, and to learn more about their lives. Sometimes I wonder if they remember me, and if they ever think about the child that grew up never knowing them.

I think that the experience of going back to your roots, learning about your history, and seeing in real life where you're from is an experience all adoptees should have. It doesn't mean that you're unhappy with the life you have now or the family you've been adopted into, it just means that you are curious about your past and want to learn more of what makes you you. If you are curious, I encourage you to make this journey, whether it's by yourself or with your family.

As I mentioned previously, I am pursuing a path to become a physical therapist. I love to work with kids and love to travel and hope to combine those interests all together. Having spent two recent summers in China volunteering with different organizations dedicated to orphan care in

China, my eyes have been opened to the orphan crisis and the immense needs that those children have. Once I am a physical therapist, I am hoping to use those skills as a tangible way to help kids with special needs and HIV/AIDS. In 10 years I would love to be working abroad in maybe a foster home setting providing therapy for children or working in a children's hospital or therapy clinic here in the USA. Eventually, I would love to get married and have kids of my own, maybe adopting a few along the way.

For others wanting to follow their journey, I encourage you to embrace your story. Learn what makes you unique—the people involved, the places you've touched. Don't be afraid to dig through emotions and thoughts, even the painful and scary ones. The events that cause one to become an orphan come from hurt and brokenness, but hope and trust can still come from that. Restoration does happen."

Richard, Adoptive Parent

Richard and his family, 2017.

"Our family has always had a special connection with China. None of our parents or grandparents had ever travelled to the country, but when we met in Bordeaux, France in 1992, Stephanie (now my wife) and I were both fascinated by Chinese culture and its fast changing society. Stephanie had studied the language and had visited China for the first time in high school. She would soon return to Shanghai to study full time for one year. To me, this was an entirely new world in which she would guide me. We would share impressions and ideas, comment on political and economic developments, discuss relentlessly about Chinese and Western prejudices until late in the night. We were eager to travel to China together, to explore the country's astonishing diversity and creativity, food, people, and embark on unique adventures in China. A long tour of seven weeks in 1995 on Chinese trains, buses, and ferries deepened our common attachment to the country. We could see the Chinese landscape endlessly unfolding along the way, and Chinese people at work everywhere, in the streets or in the fields. In the countryside, children would play on the side of the road or walk a long way to school, often by themselves. They were growing up in a rapidly changing environment. China had found a way out of poverty, but the path was not an easy one. The whole country was busy, and change was brutal.

During this long trip we became more fully aware of our common desire to start a family together. At the same time that we realised that we were ready to do so, we also learned about the sometimes terrible situation in Chinese orphanages. We spontaneously shared the same immediate feeling that to adopt a child in need of love and affection, a Chinese girl as we suspected there would be so many of them, would be deeply meaningful to us. We soon felt very strongly about this and there was no hesitation or long discussion between us. We just knew that offering a chance to one child would be a source of intense hope and happiness for us and for our whole family. Our story would later prove this to be true far beyond our expectations. Our desire for a child grew into a desire to adopt a Chinese baby girl.

Three years later, we met Xue Qi (雪琪), as she was named by the orphanage, who would become our Hannah, on August 10th, 1998, in Nanning, Guangxi. We were warmly welcomed at Mother's Love by Chan Kit Ying, Director Liu and Ms. Wu, and the staff. The building was neat and clear, lit up by the warm and bright summer sun of Southern China. We were a group of five French families coming straight from Europe, with a short stopover in Beijing and one night in a hotel in Nanning before reaching the orphanage. Although some of us had already visited China, it was the first time in Guangxi for all of us. On the flight from Beijing we could see the landscape of central China devastated by massive and deadly floods that year. With the exception of a couple of hotels, Nanning had no high-rise buildings. The city center was made up of small street markets and large avenues shaded with tall trees, and modest shops and stalls lined long bumpy roads, with the fields and green landscape in the background. The whole city was dusty, noisy, and obviously poor. We were all happy and nervous while preparing to meet the children.

At Mother's Love, the atmosphere was particularly joyful. The staff were elegantly dressed and flowers, cookies, and fruits were displayed in the reception room. Before meeting the children, Director Liu and Ms. Wu gave us a warm welcome, and Kit Ying gave a simple and intense message about the children. We were going to start a wonderful and crucial relationship with them. They were aware that they would meet their parents today. It would be emotionally challenging, and they would probably cry a lot. We would need to learn to know each other, and it would take some time. This was normal and to be expected. Patience, care, and love would progressively build the relationship between us. Stephanie and myself were moved and cheered by the message.

The doors opened, and the nurses brought the children in, all beautifully dressed. The smiles on the faces, the simple decorum of the room, the excitement of adopting families, everything converged to make that moment an intense celebration of the children. It was the very first moment of their new life, sealing our destiny as a family. We became their parents at the very same instant that they met their new family. This is probably what birth is all about: giving, receiving, and making sense of life through a common experience. As parents and children came face-to-face for the first time, our first shared emotion couldn't be more intense. Xue Qi wore a nice checked, red and yellow dress and a pair of new fancy shoes she seemed very proud of. She was intimidated by the situation (so were we), and hesitant to jump into the unknown.

There was no time to think however. As soon as Xue Qi was in our arms, she started to cry aloud, as did all the other baby girls. The room was filled with the contagious anxiety of the children and the stress of the new parents. It was time for action, hugging, babbling, and humming. Kit Ying encouraged us to leave the place quickly. We had some formalities to do anyway, so off we went, riding in a bumpy mini-bus into our life-journey.

Today Hannah is 22 years old, a bright young woman studying at the University of British Columbia in Vancouver, Canada. She particularly enjoys history, literature, traveling, playing piano, and cooking. She is interested in diplomacy, and more generally in relations between Europe and Asia, and would like to professionally contribute to this field. Nothing makes her happier than gathering with friends and family, especially when people bring experiences and souvenirs from all over the globe. Over the years, we have developed deep and friendly relations with the French families who adopted babies on the same day, and Hannah is very close to the other girls, now all in their twenties.

Hannah has a younger sister named Raphaëlle, now 19, who was not adopted. They are sisters with a very strong relationship. Both of them have charismatic personalities with very different temperaments. Their relationship has been essential to the whole family. Hannah is a wonderful older sister, always attentive and supportive. Being the elder gave her a strong sense of membership and responsibility within the family and beyond (Hannah thrived as a captain in her scouts' company when we lived in Beijing a few years ago). Raphaëlle has been admirative of and enchanted by the presence of her older sister since her first days. This relationship has contributed to building her personality as intensively happy and joyful. Hannah and Raphaëlle always stand together against difficulties and challenges.

Hannah has the most caring and appeasing temperament among the extended family and her cousins she cherishes so much. She enjoys family meetings very much and generously contributes to the dynamics and happiness of the family. By temperament she is calm and focused. Look for Hannah and you will most likely find her reading in her room. She is never late, always meticulously prepared. As a baby she was already a quiet person. She never cried at night. She enjoyed books from the first day. She would observe a lot, staring at people and scanning situations, and concentrate on what was important. I believe that she developed this capacity in her very early months, before her adoption, and probably owes much of her resilience to it. Although Hannah has a light constitution, she is physically and mentally strong. The whole family learned and benefited from this strength. Hannah may be stressed by challenges − catching trains or preparing for College exams − but never panics. She can focus very precisely on just what needs to be done, be it horse-riding, climbing, or writing essays. She never argues over petty matters. Within the family she regularly takes us back straight to the basics, attention and love among us.

Becoming Hannah's and Raphaëlle's father has been an intense experience and a blessing which has transformed my whole life. During the early months with Hannah, things were not always easy. We rapidly developed a strong relationship together, but she also had difficulties. During the early days she was prostrated and stopped walking for a while. She was quite skinny and wouldn't take much food, until we discovered she had a milk allergy and changed her diet. Back in France, Hannah would not be happy with the baby-sitter we found for her during our working hours. We could see her turning sad, silent, and inactive. These were relatively common difficulties for early-days adoption, and we fixed them like other families, each in turn, mostly with affection and the help of time. However, I still remember today one particular difficulty during those first months. At Mother's Love, Kit Ying had alerted us to the fact that adopted children usually start to build a relationship with one parent (the mother or the father), sometimes quite exclusively, before they can have a more balanced relationship with both of them. After a couple of weeks, this is exactly what happened within our family. Hannah demanded tremendous levels of affection and care, as if she was trying to fill the vacuum left from her early life, and became entirely centred on Stephanie during those days. I could understand what was going on. However, when I realised that Hannah had resolutely turned her attention away from me, and that I was unable to communicate with her, I started to doubt. I was totally engaged to become her father. But what if I failed to connect with her? What if she refused my affection? What would it mean for our family if Hannah did not consider me as her father? Those few days and moments of doubt were not long, and soon dissipated with the momentum of our new family life, but they were also intense enough that I remember them today. I realised that whatever my intentions, the love of a child should never be taken for granted. Becoming Hannah's father would also mean to be able to receive and cherish her affection, whatever and whenever she could give. Hannah's love is a unique, precious gift, and will remain so for the rest of my life.

We had the chance to live in China as a family between 2003 and 2012. In Hong Kong, where we stayed between 2003 and 2006, we first visited Kit Ying at Mother's Choice. Hannah and Raphaëlle were very young, still in their early years of primary school. We shared together the overwhelming emotion of a visit to the Child Care Home, and the mixed feelings of peace, fragility, and hope surrounding the babies quietly sleeping. The whole place was filled with subdued light and entirely arranged for the care of the children. Every person, every movement, mattered. I remember how deeply moved the two girls were by the presence of the babies, and the release of their joy as we left the room. Kit Ying accompanied us and helped to facilitate a smooth and thoughtful visit. She was well aware of the emotional challenge, the questions, as well as the true value of such a moment for visitors, especially for children. After the visit, Hannah and Raphaëlle kept asking questions about some of the babies we had seen, about adoption and abandonment in general, and about children growing up in orphanages. They wanted to return. Connecting to Mother's Choice helped them (and us as their parents) to make sense of our family and, beyond, to make sense of the life they were engaging in.

Kit Ying extended an invitation for us to visit Mother's Love in Nanning. We were all very much looking forward to this opportunity, so we spent Christmas at Mother's Love in 2004. The whole community of children, personnel, foster families, and a few visitors assembled for Christmas Eve. It was an outdoor party with barbecue and simple food and drinks. The weather was cold, and the power cut several times during the evening (power shortage was common in China at the time), leaving us with candle lights. We had brought paper and color pens for Mother's Love children. A few musicians were present, and we sang songs together, wrapped in our coats and scarfs. It was a wonderful and cheerful Christmas Eve, filled with the joy of sharing. The children were thrilled with the excitement of Christmas. We were attentive to Hannah's reaction. She was simply quiet, as ever, and happy. It was natural to be there. She enjoyed communicating with other children and sharing the affection of Kit Ying and other staff members. For the four of us, this was a profound moment for our family, one which brought us even closer together.

Hannah and Raphaëlle returned to Nanning with their mum soon after, for the 10th anniversary celebration of Mother's Love in 2005. They didn't want to miss the special milestone. They prepared songs for the party and met new friends, as other adopted children came from overseas for the celebration. They became particularly close to Fuxia (福霞), with whom they spontaneously shared much laughter and many ideas. To both of them, the Mother's Love community had become family. Raphaëlle was as thrilled as her sister to be part of it.

A few years passed before they would return again, this time in Hong Kong in July 2014. Hannah was 16, Raphaëlle 14, and they were looking for interesting activities during their summer holidays. We encouraged them to volunteer to see if and how they could help with Radiant Hope in Nanning. Kit Ying carefully considered what to propose, and arranged for a group of three children from Nanning, to come to Hong Kong for a week of vacation. With the help of two Mother's Choice staff, Hannah and Raphaëlle arranged a weeklong schedule of activities for the children in Hong Kong. They stayed with the children at Mother's Choice and accompanied them throughout the whole week—they still think of this week as a time of intense fun and excitement, and they immensely enjoyed visiting and playing together with the children. It remains puzzling to me how the group were able to communicate across language and cultural barriers—Hannah and Raphaëlle having grown up across two continents and three large cities, and the Radiant Hope children, raised in dire conditions, having never left Nanning before, and all of them struggling with AIDS—these differences didn't seem to matter at all in their communication. Quite the opposite, they seem to have played with it to build a dynamic relationship. The essence of what they shared went beyond language and across their own personal and social situations. This was a profound, formative experience for both of our girls. This time, Hannah was more deeply impressed than her sister, and she shared her reflections with us upon her return. Those few days were the best and most important vacation she had ever had, she said. She could feel that it had changed her deep inside. She had been so happy giving, sharing, and receiving with others that she felt this would inspire the rest of her life. She would think of this experience when choosing her course of study and professional activities later on.

Living in China while Hannah was a child has been an immense opportunity. We all studied Mandarin and developed a shared and deep interest for Chinese culture. We felt that it would be important that she learn Chinese, and enjoy living in the country, but I realise as I write these lines that in doing so, we were all in the same boat, and that she was never alone in the daunting task of accessing Chinese culture. Living in Hong Kong and then Beijing made it relatively easy to build and maintain our relationship with Kit Ying and Mother's Love. We know how crucial it has been for Hannah and for the shaping of her personality to be able to do this, initially together as a family, then progressively with more autonomy. What mattered was not the place of course, but the journey and the community of people who made up Mother's Love. It helped Hannah to build trust in confronting the story of her most early days, and in connecting with others. It also incorporated Mother's Love, therefore Hannah's early days, as a full part of our family story. Hannah knows it is there, as a place where she was cared and loved, and where and how to find it. Not all of her questions have an answer, but they can be asked, and there is much comfort and strength to be found in sharing. This is what we all learned in returning to Nanning, and the blessing it has brought to our whole family. This is also why her mum and I, in our secret moments, still love to call her Xue Qi."

Mei Mei, Adoptee

"My name is Mei Mei, I'm 21 years old and currently live in Copenhagen, Denmark. I was adopted when I was two years old by my mother and father, who are both doctors. Three years later, they adopted my little sister from China as well, who is 18 years old now. I'm studying to become a kindergarten teacher and I live together with my best friend and my cat. My best friend is studying to become a nurse and we've been living together for two years now. My cat is not studying anything, she just wants to eat and sleep. In my free time, I like to draw and hang out with my friends, listen to music and write. I used to sew when I was younger, too. I live a nice, quiet life with not much going on. But that, in and of itself, is more than I ever could have hoped for.

I grew up in a very nice neighbourhood in central Copenhagen. The streets were safe and there were plenty of play areas near both the schools and the after-school activities. I didn't have many friends as a child, but I did well in school and liked to draw, play pokemon and tell stories. Aside from not looking like my Caucasian parents, I might as well have been just another Danish kid.

In many ways, my childhood was ideal. I was adopted into a wealthy family and I was a bright and self-reliant child. I spoke Danish almost fluently only months after I was adopted and I left the native speakers in the dust. I was a quiet, well-adjusted kid, an 'easy' kid. I didn't ask questions about my heritage and I never cared enough to look into it either. I knew what I had to know: my parents were in Denmark and they were Danish; China was a thing of the past and therefore irrelevant to me. I never longed to find my biological parents, not because I felt anger towards them, but simply because they didn't matter. I was where I was supposed to be and I was happy. I might be in the minority about this—not wanting to have 'anything to do with my heritage'. Many of my peers asked me if I was curious and I just said no because, in retrospect, I felt detached from China and that part of me. It was not a part of me that I was very proud of because, all in all, it was just another reason why I was different.

I'm sad when I say that being adopted, whether I like it or not, has shaped my life in ways that I never thought it would. I repressed many of the negative emotions about it: the fact that my premise of being was that I was different, unwanted by my parents, and ultimately alone in a society that didn't understand me. These are big, philosophical issues that can crush a person, and I felt downtrodden when I first faced these realisations at age 18. I remember it very clearly: I was on my way home from school, sitting in the bus and looking out the window. I had been fighting with my parents that morning and I still felt this anger inside of me that felt like it could tear me apart. At that point I realised that it wasn't normal, but I also realised that I didn't deserve to feel that way.

I became determined not to be dictated by anger and sadness, and I started going to a psychologist who specialised in working with adopted children. It was a very tough time in my life, but also the most fruitful. There are issues I still struggle with until this day, but I'm forever grateful to myself for doing it. I was never someone who thought I'd ever need a therapist or psychologist, but the truth is, anyone can benefit from seeing one. You have to be willing to face your inner demons, and that's the hard part of it. For me, I had to let go of a lot of animosity. It wasn't directed at anyone in particular, but I had been, for a long time, ignoring the circumstances of my childhood. And then, when I finally faced the reality of my abandonment, I was livid. Being 18 and having your whole foundation shaken like that was a horrible experience. Most days I felt like screaming at the sky, as rain poured on my face and lightning went off in the background, like it does in the movies. I went for a long time thinking the world had been unfair to me, that I deserved better and that nothing good had come from the life that I had been given.

It might seem dramatic, but it was the reality I lived with. It was a perception of my existence that deeply touched me, and overcoming that rift in order to better myself wasn't an easy feat. But I did it. It took me years, but now I can't imagine not having done it. But it was a crazy thing to realise that the reason I was so self-reliant, mature, and stand-offish, was because I was scared of people seeing the real me. I pushed people away and never let them in because I expected to be abandoned and discarded in the end anyway. I had been living for 18 years like that without ever questioning this belief! I felt like Will Smith from the Fresh Prince of Bel-Air because my life had been thoroughly flip-turned upside down.

Through hard work, introspection, and perseverance, I can proudly say that I have chosen kindness and love to be things that guide me, the beacon after which I steer my ship. It leads me to better paths, more fun, more friends, more happiness than I ever thought I'd experience. I've learned to love myself and repair what was broken so many years ago when I was left at that train station in the middle of the night. And most importantly I've learned to forgive. And in these actions, this path, I've become the person I've always wanted to be. If you had asked me just 3 years ago if I'd ever be this happy, I probably would have said no. But here I am. And I'm truly, so, so happy.

I never knew much about Guangxi when I was younger because it simply wasn't a part of my life. Guangxi and China in general were concepts that I had no relation to. I didn't ask questions and I never looked into it before my family and I went there in 2011 to visit Mother's Love, my foster home, and my little sister's orphanage.

That visit was one of the most impactful experiences in my whole life. For the first time in 15 years, I found myself fitting in perfectly. No one looked at me strangely in the streets, no one minded what I was doing as much as they minded my white, Scandinavian parents. It was a feeling I had never felt before and it's something that most of us who are adopted, rarely get to feel: complete anonymity. In Denmark, I had experienced many microaggressions and racial slurs directed towards me, phrases like "go back to China" and "ching chong konnichiwa". But there, in Guangxi, there was no such problem at all. I felt right at home.

The most important part of my visit was, of course, the visit to see my foster parents. We had been in contact for many years via letters that Kit Ying translated for us and forwarded to them, but it was the first time that I would get to meet them and see the place where I had lived for a year. I remember being so excited and nervous, I thought I was going to throw up. I can't possibly describe the feeling of vague recognition I felt when we pulled up in the driveway to a small row of houses. It was during the summer but the fields were barren, and the houses were simple and plain. There were a few chicken coops outside the houses.

I'll never forget how familiar it felt to see my foster parents and the home where I had lived. They were extremely hospitable and as they showed us around their humble home I felt flashes of something familiar, but couldn't put my finger on. It felt like a faint scent of something familiar, gone all too soon when you try to identify it. We all had lunch together and my foster mother showed us pictures of when she had first gotten me. Until that point, we had never seen pictures of me as a baby—I had always been at least one and a half years old, sporting a frown and pigtails. But there I was, fat and wrapped in three layers of pink knit, hairless and pouting in her arms. Imagine never having seen pictures of yourself as a baby before, and suddenly seeing yourself like that for the first time at the age of 15. I tell you, it's wild.

My foster mother told us small tidbits about me as a child, like how I would refuse to jump over puddles in the streets, and instead waited patiently until someone came and carried me over them. One of the most amazing facts she shared with me was that her eldest son was the reason I first started to draw. I have drawn all my life, it's my absolute favourite hobby, but I hadn't realised that it had started when her son would hand me a pencil and a piece of paper after he came home from school, and that I'd lie on the floor drawing while he finished his homework.

Getting to know all of that, experience all of it, has given me so much. I've made great memories there, I've been so happy and I've learned so much. That's why Guangxi has a special place in my heart, even if I live so far away.

When I think of Mother's Love, the first thing that comes to my mind is the large statue that stood in the middle of the garden. I think many of us who are adopted from there will remember the white statue of a woman laying on her side with a baby, reminding everyone what they're trying to achieve, what's awaiting the children they're caring for. I had always thought it was such a beautiful statue, and now that I'm older, I appreciate it even more. It's a very powerful symbol and a wonderful reminder.

When my family and I visited China again in 2011, Mother's Love had already closed, and the building was ready to be torn down. I was very lucky to be able to see that statue once again, even though it was from a distance. The grass on the lawn had grown taller, and half of the buildings behind the statue had already been taken down. The sight didn't make me sad as much as it made me wistful. I was happy that Mother's Love had achieved what it had set out to do and bettered so many lives, including mine, in the process. Even so, it was one of my favourite monuments of all time that was going to be gone soon.

Mei Mei, me, and her younger sister.

We also met with the wonderful Kit Ying, who has helped my family in so many ways throughout the years—keeping in contact with my foster family for us by translating our letters and so much more. It fills my heart with overwhelming joy to know that there are people like her out there, in the world, doing so much good for so many people. I'm so grateful that Mother's Love has been a part of my life. And I'm even more grateful that the people there will continue to change people's lives for the better.

My dream has always been to become a happy person and to make others happy as well. I want to make sure that others are safe and well, to care for those who might need it. I want to give everything I have to offer to the people around me, and I am confident that I will be able to do it. I hope to be working with children in need, whether that be in a kindergarten, school yard, or home. I want children to know that they'll be able to overcome anything.

I hope that whoever reads my story knows that they can be happy as well, and that, no matter how bad and how hopeless things might seem, they can be the beacon of light that bursts through the darkness and leads the way towards happiness. There is so much beauty and joy in this world, but we must keep our heads high to see it. And once we've seen it, once we've embraced it, we, ourselves, become it. And we all deserve that."

Natalie, Adoptee

"My name is Natalie Xià Měi Henes. I was born in August 1992, most likely in a small community just outside of Nanning, China, and brought to an orphanage by bike. I was left in an abandoned room with a wet umbilical cord, and luckily Kit Ying found me. As the story goes, she immediately knew exactly who to call and connected me with wonderful parents who were living in Bronxville, New York. They came with my maternal grandparents to adopt me when I was only a couple months old. Throughout the trip and the first few years of my life, my grandparents compiled thousands of pictures in albums that documented the journey to get me and the love that surrounded me.

A few years later, my parents adopted a boy from Hong Kong and named him Xavier. Although I did not know what to expect, I wanted to name him "Chopsticks". We went to Hong Kong to get him. According to my parents, it was a whole different experience than when they came to get me. Xavier and I have made great memories having snowball fights in the driveway, skiing in upstate New York, and multiple road trips around the states. I could not have asked for a better sibling to make our little family whole.

I attended an excellent Catholic grade schools in Bronxville, New York and all-girls high schools in New York and Arizona. In the summer of my junior year of high school, I took an eye-opening trip back to China to reunite with Kit Ying. I spent time at Mother's Love with the little ones who had HIV or AIDS and the children who had mental and physical disabilities. The smiles on their faces would light up a room. We played games, painted nails, and completed an "I Spy" project. Even though there was a large language barrier, this life-changing trip would later on influence my studies in school.

Natalie (front) with her adoptive mother, Beverly, visiting children with special needs at Mother's Love.

I attended college at the University of Arizona in Tucson, Arizona. I thought I wanted to major in business or Asian Studies, but the classes didn't appeal to me. Understanding me well, my mom suggested I try education. I was intrigued and recalled my experience in China a few years ago. I became an Arizona State University Sun Devil at the Mary Lou Fulton Teachers College and graduated with dual certification in Elementary and Special Education with magna cum laude honors. I also joined the Kappa Alpha Theta sorority and met my best friends there. The sorority is a network of smart, driven women of which I am so proud to say that I am an alumna. Currently, I am an elementary teacher in Scottsdale, Arizona and continuing my Master's education through online classes. I am only in my fourth year of teaching, but I plan to be in the classroom shaping young minds for many years.

In my 25 years of life, I have traveled to many of the 50 states in the US, Mexico, Costa Rica, and overseas to China and Europe. My parents have created a love of travel in me. I want to meet new people, see the sites, and experience other cultures in the world. I look forward to seeing more in the future.

I have been so fortunate to have loving parents who have shown me the numerous opportunities in the world, given me an invaluable education, and supported me through all of the ups and downs in my life. Without Kit Ying knowing the perfect family to place me with, I would not be the woman I am today, so I am incredibly indebted to her and my biological parents, who I may never know, but wanted a better life for me."

Samuel, Adoptee

"My name is Samuel Yung. I am currently attending Venice High School, a public school in Los Angeles, California, and I enjoy learning about history, math, science, and English. I also like going to basketball games, football games, and hanging out with friends at my school. My family is great. My parents are both second-generation Chinese-American. We attend a church called Evergreen Baptist Church, in San Gabriel, California. My parents brought me here when I was 12 years old. Since then, I have been adjusting to the culture and ways of American life pretty well.

Samuel, 2013.

I was born in Nanning, China, and when I think of that place, I think of all the wonderful memories of being with friends from Mother's Love and being able to roam around the place without a lot of cars and with a lot of greenery. I think of the Chinese New Year holidays, where we got to play with firecrackers and received red envelopes from *ayis* and their relatives. I think of the barbeques we always had on Christmas night, when we got to leave school early, and received presents afterwards. I remember being able to stay at many different aunties' houses during the holidays and playing with their children and letting them take care of me. When I was a kid, I remember the teams of volunteers from Evergreen Baptist Church who came to serve Mother's Love. What I remember the most about those visits were all those times I got to spend with Uncle Victor (the team leader) and the time we went horseback riding. I also recall all the times I spent with Kailee (one of my friends from Mother's Love) in Hong Kong when we traveled there for medical checks, especially when we went to Hong Kong Disneyland. With all of those fun and memorable things coming to mind, I am also reminded that it is a place where my biological parents left me, and they are probably still there, maybe wondering what had happened to me.

To me, China is a place where I received so many blessings, but it is also a place of hurt from being abandoned at a young age and later bullied by some mean kids at school because of my disability. It is also a place that shaped me into who I am today; no matter whether the result is perfect or terrible, it changed me in little ways as I walked through life in China.

While attending public school in China, I struggled a lot because of the opinions of my classmates and how they treated me. A lot of kids at school bullied me because of my disability but thankfully, it did not go far. I think they also bullied me because I did not have a biological mother or father to take care of me, and I always felt different from the rest of the kids in the school. These experiences developed hatred in my heart, to the point that I even wanted to go back one day and take my revenge. When I first arrived in the US, our family had a hard time getting along, partly because I was so angry all the time. But as I gave it more and more to God, I began to feel the freedom of forgiveness. Through this process, I also changed to become more obedient to my parents and my sense of hatred lessened. I still struggle with this problem occasionally, but as I rely more on God, he continues to make me better.

Growing up I always enjoyed hanging out with my friends at Mother's Love. I liked to do different activities together, but also just talk and share about lives with each other. I still recall the times when my friend David (振山) and I, as little kids, would sneak out of bed in the middle of the night and talk about what we did during the day and share jokes with each other. Occasionally, we would also sneak around the boys' room looking for things to do, and when the *ayis* entered the room, we would run to our beds as fast as possible, getting caught once in a while. I also remember playing and spending time with two other friends Charley and Eddie after they moved back to Mother's Love (after spending some time living in foster homes). I especially remember being able to hang out with Charley the night before I left to meet my adopted parents.

I wish to be able to return to see how the place that I once lived looks like now, and see my friends that I once played with, especially those that I met when I stayed in the Nanning state orphanage. I am excited to travel back, but also I am not sure of how my old friends and those *ayis* who once took care of me would feel about seeing me returning. I am also afraid of not being able to adapt to how I lived like in the past, since I've gotten used to life in America with my family and new friends. With all the gifts and blessings that God has showered upon me, I am also driven to help those who might be in need, whether it is locally in the homeless shelters or abroad helping people who are less fortunate than I am now.

I have not gone back since I came to America, but I will most likely go back and visit Nanning at some point. Although I have seen some pictures taken by Uncle Gerry and Auntie Irene when they went back for the closing of Mother's Love a few years ago. I think those of us who had lived at Mother's Love should go back because it's a part of us, even if we were adopted as little babies. Connecting back with the place where we grew up is a very good thing. It can be very uplifting just to see how far you have come, to give thanks for all the things people have done for you, and to give back what others have given to you.

I do not know what I will do ten years from now, but I think I will probably be an adult working somewhere in the business world in America. I will probably be living in an apartment in America, because the price for buying a house here is so expensive. I think that I will still be in California, but I am not sure whether I will move away from my current home or not. I hope that I will still be a Christian and that I will hold firm to God in times of turmoil and times of success. He will be my guide as I go about my day and help me to be a godlier man as I go about my work and everyday chores. I hope that I will be able to afford a dog, because I have always liked dogs, even when I was living in China. I am not sure whether I will date or get married or not, but I hope that I will be able to adopt kids from around the world, especially those kids that are living in countries that are in desperate conditions.

I want to tell those who are still living in the orphanages in China to not give up and lose hope, even though things are tough. Continue to fight on in the orphanage; do not give up because it is hard, but remember your helper Jesus and continue to fight on using the strength He gives you."

Shao Qing, Nurse

"What is love? Through living in the big family of Mother's Love, I realized that love is acceptance, love is kind, love takes companionship, love creates inheritance, love enables me to keep moving forward.

Time flies. As I tried to recall my 18 years working at Mother's Love, everything remains as vivid as if it just happened yesterday. I can still hear the babies crying. They were crying to be cared for and crying to survive. By responding to all those cries of the babies, all of us who worked at Mother's Love learned the definition of love and the value of a life. It was an unforgettable experience to watch those crying little babies recover to health under our care, and one after another, they went home with their adoptive parents. We witnessed the life transformation because of love. Out of love, we served the crying babies. Out of love, the babies became healthy again. Out of love, their adoptive parents came to take them home. Out of love, they grew into healthy and amazing young women. This miracle of love also transformed us, those of us who served the children. Day by day, our hearts filled with the wonders of love.

Shao Qing with babies at Mother's Love, 1996.

Fushi (福时), the last child we received at Mother's Love, was born with congenital heart disease. Her lips and skin were constantly pale, but she was a pretty little girl who enjoyed our love and loved us. She died at the age of two. However, she died in the loving arms of her beloved child care worker. In the same season, Mother's Love also fulfilled its mission and closed down the local services. And all of us were ready to move forward in a new stage of life.

There were 11 children with severe disabilities who were not adopted before we closed Mother's Love. Settling them into a new home was one of the biggest challenges we had ever encountered. First of all, due to their severe disabilities, our child care workers who had accompanied them over the years had developed an intimate understanding of their needs—we knew it would be hard for the children to adjust to the separation and change in caregivers. Many of our child care workers were willing to follow the children back to the state orphanage and continue to provide care and love to them. In the end, the state orphanage agreed to receive all of our children with special needs and hired their caregivers so that our children could start their new lives while minimizing change in their daily lives. We believe that every single one of our children is in God's plan and living under the His cover.

During this transition, I started to search for my next step in life. I went through many struggles while considering my career path. Eventually, I decided to devote myself to the same community that I had been serving at Mother's Love. In November 2013, I joined World Vision to continue serving orphans with special needs. It's been five years since I joined World Vision. When I look back at the path I took, I see the ups and downs that I had to go through to follow my calling and life mission, but I am glad that I never gave up or regretted my decision.

I can't remember how many times I was asked why I chose a career with such a low income. Each time, I just smile. In my heart, I believe that this is God's plan for my life, and he has been faithful in providing for me and blessing my life. His grace equips me to keep moving forward.

Nowadays, God continues to choose me as His servant. There is a significant purpose in my career. I just embrace this mission with a smile and open arms. In the coming five years, I will take on a leadership position. I will learn to be a leader to lead the team, to train, and to coach. I will also be responsible for developing a child-centered service model. The spirit and the legend of Mother's Love lives in me, and my role is to continue this legend and pass on God's love. It's an undeniable truth that God's love for us never changes."

Afterword:
To the Children of
Mother's Love

As we reach the conclusion of this book, evoking these many memories makes me even more fully aware of the importance of each and every person—every child, colleague, or individual in the community—that I had the chance to encounter during my years in Guangxi. During that time, Mother's Love cared for around 1,500 children, of which 1,400 were adopted, largely by overseas families. Let me finish by addressing these young men and women, many of whom are now young adults, and some are even parents.

To the dear children of Mother's Love, my wish is that as you read this book, it will inspire you to start or continue your journey to discover who you are, and where you came from. Through *Hidden Treasures*, I have done my best to put down into words the story of Mother's Love, and the context that surrounded it. The realities as described in this book are at times difficult to face, but I chose to be as honest as possible, fully believing that you have the right as well as the strength required to know. Although China in the 1990s was rife with poverty and the conditions were often terrible, you come from a small and modest place in Nanning that was full of light and love. At Mother's Love, you were cared for by a team of loving and dedicated individuals who shared a deep commitment to the Nanning community and found their life's meaning in serving children. I want you to know that you were and continue to be deeply loved by the Mother's Love community, and that each of your lives is from its beginning unique and precious.

While I've tried to articulate as best as I can this part of your history and identity, you may still have a lot of questions. Mother's Love was a place filled with love, but I also recognize that the circumstances that led to the founding of Mother's Love are filled with loss and grief, and that in spite of all the details I have tried to include in this book, that you will still have questions to which I simply don't have the answers.

I encourage you to process those questions in community—whether that be your family and loved ones, other adoptees who share similar experiences, or those of us who were closely involved with Mother's Love. Although Mother's Love no longer exists as an organization and as a physical building, it's spirit lives on through the community of staff (many of whom continue to work passionately in the area of children's welfare and protection in Nanning and beyond) and families whose lives were touched by Mother's Love. This community is alive and well, and we welcome you to reach out to us through Mother's Choice in Hong Kong (www.motherschoice.org) and the alumni network attached to it. We may not have all the answers, but we are here to walk alongside you if you so choose. I am convinced that making these simple connections and being in community are invaluable as you continue along your journey.

Over the years, I have been asked a lot of 'why' questions—why I stayed in Nanning, why I chose to take a baby out of the state orphanage, why I started Mother's Love, why I arranged for the babies to be adopted overseas. The most honest answer is that I had witnessed something I couldn't unsee, and I just couldn't turn away. I had never planned to stay in Nanning, never devised a strategy on how I could make a difference to the crisis unfolding in China—my actions were driven by the call for help from each precious life in front of me, from one human to another. At that time, I didn't have a lot of time to think or to ask myself too many questions, I simply responded to the babies in the state orphanage, whose eyes watched me as I walked into the room and spoke deeply into my heart. I did my best in the situation, and from that, I rest satisfied.

While this is the end of the book, this is by no means the end of the story. It continues on in the future that you chart for yourself in the years to come. Your time at Mother's Love is a very real part of your past, but it doesn't define your future. Most of you are entering into adulthood and are beginning to articulate the complexities of what your adoption and your Chinese heritage mean to your identity. Each of your stories is unique, and I hope that you will contribute to the growing voices of adoptees around the world to shape the conversation around adoption and the care of children in need. Adoption systems around the world are far from perfect, and I believe that by sharing your story and your perspective, you can help to mold the way we as a community serve adoptees, no matter your stage of life.

I believe that each of us is called to respond to the needs or challenges of our generation, in big ways and in small ways, and it's up to us to decide if and how we will respond. In my own life, it was seeing the abandoned babies in the Nanning state orphanage in 1992, and choosing to respond in the way I knew how—by picking up that first baby girl and carrying her out of the orphanage. To some, it may have seemed a brave move, but I know that I was able to take that step and many others that came after because of the guidance, encouragement, and nurturing of individuals in my life. My work was simply a continuation of those who came before me, I simply picked up the baton to continue the work of building a better future for the next generation. I hope that when the challenges of your generation come knocking, that you, too, will be compelled to action. I hope that you will take comfort knowing that you are not alone, that you come from a community of individuals who have dedicated their lives to building a better future so that you, too, can one day build a better future for the generations who come after you. This story is now yours to continue.

With love,
Auntie Kit Ying
July 2019

Acknowledgements

I would like to thank the following people:

My family by birth

and

My spiritual family and community who set a great model for me to follow. I especially honor those who are already in heaven: Grandma Holt, Dr. David Kim, Molly Holt, and Dawn Gage.

The founders of Mother's Choice, Ranjan & Phyllis Marwah, Gary & Helen Stephens. Without your courage and faith to start Mother's Choice, the stories of Mother's Love would not be possible.

My mentors, David & Carol Boyd, who were the first to draw me out, affirmed and invested in my leadership potential, and continue to walk alongside me even up to now.

All my co-workers around the world, especially Christine Sams, Michelle Ruetschle, Chan Yuk Ling, Cheng Yu Pei, Wu Mei Hui, John & Jane Stoke, David & Jenny McKechnie, Joyce Lu, Ross & Raewyn Meredit, and Kerry & Angela Hartley. There is no measure for your physical presence, friendship, and partnership. You are truly like a family to me.

The Government leadership of Guangxi Civil Affairs from 1992 – 2003. Without your caring and courageous hearts to invite Mother's Choice to partner together, the transformation of across the Guangxi state orphanages would not be possible.

Pastor Cory Ishida & the family of Evergreen Baptist Church SGV who committed to journey with me and the children at Mother's Love unconditionally despite our ups and downs throughout the years.

Richard Balme, Jennifer Cheng, Serrie Fung who generously contributed their time and talent to walk this journey with me. You not only believed that this story was worth being told, but that it must be told.

Kiet Van who used his artistic talent to bring my manuscript to life.

Appendix

1. Mother's Love Memorial Garden

Foster parents grieving at the memorial service for their foster child, Yong Ju (邕菊), 2004.

Although the Mother's Love memorial garden no longer exists, we still remember the babies and children who passed away while under care at Mother's Love. We have included their names here as a tribute to them.

福利 Fu Li
吴早 Wu Zao
柳文珂 Liu Wen Ke
柳文车 Liu Wen Che
莉莉 Li Li
邕菊 Yong Ju
碧羿 Bi Yi
郁小童 Yu Xiao Tong
文建珠 Wen Jian Zhu
思蓓 Si Bei
岑福时 Cen Fu Shi
陳妹 Chan Mei
黨幼珍 Dang You Zhen
岑福時 Cen Fu Shi
岑福陶 Cen Fu Tao
金燕初 Jin Yan Chu
李陽 Li Yang
柳謝恩 Lou Die En
民彩秋 Min Cai Qiu
民盛瓊 Min Sheng Qiong
謝港 Xie Gang
院彩莉 Yuan Can Li
院嬋邯 Yuan Chan Han
院華倩 Yuan Hua Qian
院沛沛 Yuan Pei Pei
院樂成 Yuan Le Cheng
院小明 Yuan Xiao Ming
院秀君 Yuan Xiu Jun
院云光 Yuan Yun Guang
愛春燕 Ai Chun Yan
院云寧 Yuan Yun Ning

Precious Group
衛娟 Wei Juan
陽照 Yang Zhao
冠美 Guan Mei
亞當 Ya Dang
冬雪 Dong Xue

2. Child Abandonment and Adoption in China

Until 1949 China was a society with profound social hierarchies and inequalities. It was plagued with extreme poverty and lack of access to the most basic living conditions for the vast majority of the population. The poorest were the most exposed to malnutrition or starvation, pandemics, and the absence of healthcare and education. Many children were left orphaned and homeless as a consequence of the early death of their parents resulting from poverty. Beyond this, Chinese society, as other traditional societies before they modernized, did not view children as full individuals equivalent to adults, with proper rights to dignity and personal development as is common today. Bearing children was not primarily understood by parents as a path to emotional accomplishment and happiness, but rather as a duty to be performed to secure the economic subsistence and transmission of the family's identity. In a rural and labor-intensive economy, the children would help and progressively take over with labor in the fields. The oldest son would inherit the land and take care of the parents in their older age. Girls would need to receive a dowry to negotiate a good marriage before leaving the family. Customary law would not allow them to inherit from their parents.

With dire economic conditions, procreation was an essential aspect of social life in the entire population, with decisive consequences for parents as well as for children. In such a context, not all babies were equally welcome by families. Failing to deliver a son would mean the extinction of the lineage and severe difficulties for parents as they aged. Failing to marry off a daughter on the other hand could mean a burden for the entire household. A child with a handicap would be a tremendous social and economic challenge. There was therefore a strong and exclusive preference for boys and for healthy children among families. Whatever their affection, in front of tradition and customary law, parents would desperately need a son. This tradition is still vivid in today's rural China, and largely continues to shape parenthood and family life of the whole population in a more urban and modernized context since the foundation of the PRC.[30]

---

30. Johnson (Kay Ann), *Wanting a Daughter, Needing a Son. Abandonment, Adoption and Orphanage Care in China*. Edited by Amy Lkatzkin. Minneapolis, Yeong and Yeong, 2004. http://fortune.com/2015/11/02/china-one-child-policy/

In 1950, before the decline during the Great Leap Forward, the total fertility rate in China was above 6 children per woman. Women would go through multiple pregnancies while maternal, perinatal, and infant mortality was very high. Death commonly accompanied birth, and people were accustomed to losing many babies. These harsh conditions explain how parents could be pushed or forced by circumstances to sometimes select the children they would raise. Unfortunately, abandonment and infanticide of baby girls and handicapped children were common practices.[31]

In parallel, institutions caring for orphans and abandoned children existed in China long before the founding of the PRC in 1949. In the South, such welfare institutions were organized by benevolent associations established by clans or extended families, often financed through farmland endowments. Elsewhere, charities funded by wealthy individuals provided assistance on a more limited scale. Beginning in the 19th Century, and more intensively after 1860 when the treaties ending the Second Opium War with France and the UK opened up the entire country to missionary activity, the number of Catholic and Protestant institutions expanded dramatically and played a primary role in caring for orphans. Finally, although this reality is frequently overlooked, Chinese families themselves would frequently welcome children through some forms of customary adoption, as they still do in the country today.[32] All this was far however to cover the needs of those who were orphaned, abandoned, or neglected as a result of poverty.

After a long period of chaos leading to the collapse of the Empire in 1911, the history of China in the 20th century was plagued with imperialism, civil war and revolution. While the population was confronted with a succession of disasters generating heavy casualties, displacements, and persisting deep poverty, social institutions were also shattered. After the 1949 revolution, the land reform eradicated the financial power of rural clans, while the nationalization of business annihilated the possibility for private philanthropy. Privately financed charities were deprived of their economic basis. Foreign missions were

---

31. Mungelo (D.E.), *Drowning Girls in China. Female Infanticide since 1650*. New York, Rowman and Littlefield, 2008. King (Michelle T.), *Between Birth and Death. Female Infanticide in 19th Century China*. Stanford, Stanford University Press, 2014.
32. Johnson (Kay Ann), *China's Hidden Children. Abandonment, Adoption, and the Human Costs of the One-Child Policy*. The University of Chicago Press, 2016.

expelled from the country, leading many of them to settle in Hong Kong or Taiwan.[33] They would only progressively return after the end of the Cultural Revolution in 1976. The socialist government of the PRC instituted instead the Ministry of Civil Affairs,[34] which would oversee Child Welfare Institutes (儿童福利院) and a larger number of Social Welfare Institutes (社会福利院) where orphans, disabled, and needy elderly would be hosted in the same compound.[35]

When the one-child policy was introduced in 1979, China was still in a state of deep poverty with very minimal welfare institutions provided by the State and work units. They were rapidly overwhelmed by the massive waves of infant abandonment when the policy was actively implemented in the 1980s and 1990s. Foreign reports revealed the brutality of the one-child policy, the deadly discrimination against baby girls, and the appalling situation in the state orphanages where mortality was very high, shocking the international community.[36] The introduction of international adoption would help to face the crisis, and the Chinese authorities progressively professionalized the management of orphanages and encouraged adoption as part of larger social welfare development,[37] fortunately leaving the situation of the 1990s described here as an atrocity of the past.

The current Adoption Law (中华人民共和国收养法) was passed in 1991, and revised in 1998.[38] Adoption in China is under supervision of the China Centre for Children's Welfare and Adoption (CCCWA) (中国儿童福利和收养中心). New guidelines for international adoption were

---

33. While foreign missionaries were expelled, many Chinese Christians remained in China and continued to develop community activities.
34. The Ministry of Civil Affairs, in charge of population at the national, provincial and county level of government.
35. This was the situation of the Nanning State Orphanage.
36. *The Dying Rooms*. BBC TV Report, 1995. Human Rights Watch/Asia, *Death by Default. A Policy of Fatal Neglect in China State Orphanages*. New York, Human Rights Watch, January 1996.
37. A good analysis of the policies dealing with orphan children can be found in Shang (Xiaoyuan), Fisher (Karen R.), *Caring for Orphan Children in China*. New York, Lexington Books, 2014.
38. Adoption Law of the People's Republic of China was adopted at the 23rd Meeting of the Standing Committee of the Seventh National People's Congress and promulgated by Order No. 54 of the President of the People's Republic of China on December 29, 1991, amended in accordance with the Decision on Revising the Adoption Law of the People's Republic of China adopted at the 5th Meeting of the Standing Committee of the Ninth National People's Congress on November 4, 1998.

released in 2007. According to statistics from the Ministry of Civil Affairs Statistical Yearbook in 2014, 525,179 orphans were registered by the government (23,701 in Guangxi), 22,772 couples registered to adopt a child (1,624 in Guangxi), and 22,876 children were adopted (1,621 in Guangxi), the vast majority of them by Chinese citizens.[39] These numbers show a significant decline in adoption since the year 2000 when a peak of 56,191 children adopted was reached.

Figure 1: Adoption in the PRC 1999-2012

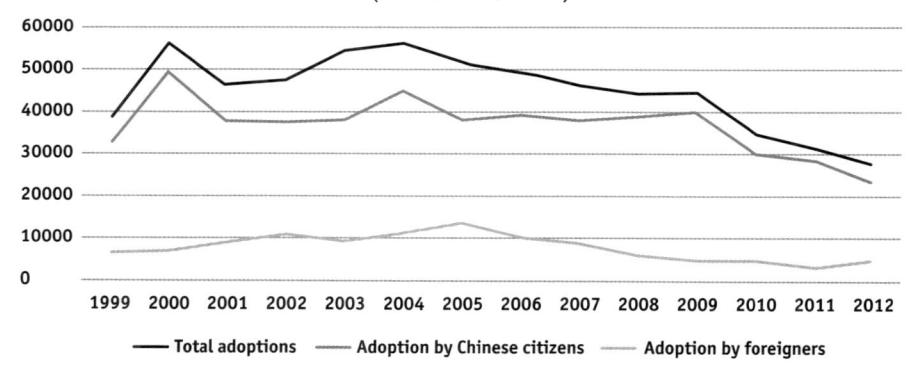

Figure 1: Adoption in the PRC 1999-2012

39. Source: Ministry of Civil Affairs Statistical Yearbook, various years.

Table 1: Adoption in Guangxi 1999-2012

(Source: Ministry of Civil Affairs Statistical Yearbook, various years from 2000 to 2016).

Year	Total adoptions	Adopted by Chinese citizens	Adopted by foreigners
1999	38019	31882	6137
2000	56191	49500	6691
2001	4584	37200	8644
2002	47860	37200	10218
2003	54159	37642	9275
2004	55572	44708	10864
2005	50921	38057	12864
2006	49148	39325	9724
2007	46047	37790	8257
2008	44115	38617	5498
2009	44359	39964	4395
2010	34473	29978	4495
2011	31329	28117	3212
2012	27310	23169	4141

3. Children's Rights in China

The PRC Constitution provides for the state protection of children, and prohibits maltreatment of children. Among many laws and regulations protecting children's rights, the primary Law in this field is The People's Republic of China Law on the Protection of Minors (中国末成年人保护法), first passed in 1991 and revised in 2006, which entered into force on June 1, 2007. This Law sets up responsibilities of families, schools, and the government with regard to the protection of children's rights, and judicial protection as well.

Major international documents relating to children's rights that the PRC government has signed and ratified are as follows:

- UN Convention on the Rights of the Child 1989 (CRC) (Entry into force for China: April 1, 1992);

- Optional Protocol to the Convention on the Rights of Child on the Sale of Children, Child Prostitution, and Child Pornography 2000 (Entry into force for China: January 3, 2003);

- International Covenant on Economic, Social and Cultural Rights 1966 (Entry into force for China: June 27, 2001);

- The Convention on the Elimination of All Forms of Discrimination Against Women 1979 (Entry into force for China: December 3, 1981);

- Worst Forms of Child Labour Convention 1999 (Entry into force for China: August 8, 2003);

- The Hague Convention on the Protection of Children and Cooperation in Respect of Intercountry Adoption 1993 (Receipt of Instrument: September 16, 2005).

It is worth noting that when deciding on ratification of the UN Convention on the Rights of the Child, the PRC Standing Committee of the National People's Congress (NPC, China's top legislative body) made a reservation to Article 6 on the inherent right to life, stating that China

shall fulfil its obligation provided by this article under the prerequisite of planned birth provided by Article 25 of the PRC Constitution.
Source: Library of Congress
https://www.loc.gov/law/help/child-rights/china.php
Accessed August 12, 2017.

4. The One-Child Policy (独生子女政策)

The One-Child Policy is the name commonly given to the policy of birth control adopted by the PRC between 1979 and 2015. It is arguably the largest population planning policy ever adopted by a government, and as such the object of many important controversies related to its philosophy and implementation.

Governments usually encourage their population to grow for philosophical, economic, and political reasons. Population size is indeed commonly understood as a source of economic wealth and national influence, while birth planning is left to the decision and the freedom of the parents. However, population size is not always equivalent to prosperity. In China, misery has often been associated with the incapacity of the country to control its demographics. With a population of 1,388,995,602 in 2017, China is the most populated country in the world. It feeds 19% of the world population with less than 10% of the world's total arable land. The demography pressures natural resources available for development. Therefore the question of controlling the size of the population was soon considered by the PRC, in order to relieve pressure on natural resources available for development. Early steps were initiated during the Maoist period, and the population planning policy came to full formulation with the one-child policy introduced in 1979. The policy included the limitation to one child for each family, the subjection of maternity to age and social conditions, forced abortions, female and male sterilizations, implanted contraception procedures, denunciation and fines imposed against contravening families, and deprivation of rights for hidden children *de facto* left without a legal status.[40] The policy was implemented at the provincial and local, village level, and revised several times. In its latest formulation, it included several significant

---

40. For an in-depth review see Greenhalgh (Susan), Winckler (Edwin A.), *Governing China's Population. From Leninist to Neoliberal Biopolitics*. Stanford, Stanford University Press, 2005.

exemptions, including for ethnic minorities which were not subject to birth limitations. In 2007, 36% of China's population was subject to a strict one-child restriction, with an additional 53% being allowed to have a second child if the first child was a girl. Parents who were themselves both single children could also claim to a second child.

The policy was implemented in several waves, generating a whole bureaucracy and structuring an in-depth relationship between the government and the population. While China was opening up its economy and its mentality, the one-child policy administered the most intimate and emotional behavior of the people in a very top-down and coercive way, through population control in neighborhoods and workplaces. While the population ignored or resisted the injunctions of the policy, the government launched large Maoist-style campaigns, intended to deliver quantitative results through active and commonly brutal implementation. The data presented below show that the implementation of the one-child policy reached its first peak in 1983, about which few reports and observations are available,[41] and a second one in 1991, just before the baby abandonment crisis as witnessed in Guangxi.

While several factors converge to explain infant abandonment and the situation of orphanages in China in the 1990s, including traditional mentalities, economic modernization, internal work migration and poor administration, the one-child policy implementation transformed an existing social problem into a massive crisis of unprecedented scale and intensity. It exacerbated the preference for baby boys at birth and the blame for parents bearing additional children. It pushed parents to renounce to give birth or to conceal the life of their new born babies to avoid social humiliation (families giving birth to more than one child were publicly denounced and legally penalized). It forced women refusing abortion and scared by the promise of sterilization to dissimulate their pregnancies, to give birth in hazardous conditions, and to hide or abandon children born in illegality. The surge of infant abandonment, rather than resulting from poverty or migration, largely evolved as the institutional and social pressure of the population planning policy. Beyond the peaks of the abandonment crisis, this has been the ordinary experience of Chinese families, and the painful condition of Chinese women for two

---

41. A narrative of the creation of a private orphanage by local people in Jinsha, Hubei province, at the end of the 1980s, can be found in Sang Ye, *China Candid. The People on the People's Republic*. Edited by Geremie R. Barmé, with Miriam Lang. Berkeley, the University of California Press, 2006, pp. 87-106.

generations. While the Chinese population generally accepted the policy, it is also well aware of the sacrifices that came with it.

The policy continues to generate controversy.[42] According to the Chinese authorities, 400 million births were prevented. The fertility rate in China has indeed fallen from 6.11 in 1955 to 3.01 in 1980 and 1.56 in 2017. However, White and al. for instance claim that "as much as three-quarters of the decline in fertility since 1970 occurred before the launching of the one-child policy; fertility levels fluctuated in China after the policy was launched; and most of the further decline in fertility since 1980 can be attributed to economic development, not coercive enforcement of birth limits."[43] Between 1980 and 1988, the total fertility rate (TFR) even increased against the implementation of the one-child policy. The new push in enforcement of the policy at the beginning of the 1990s has to be understood in this perspective. Comparisons with other countries in Asia (Japan, Hong Kong, or Thailand) suggest that the demographic transition (the transition from high birth rates and high infant mortality rates in poorer countries to low birth rates and low infant mortality rates in richer countries) in China has not been necessarily faster with the one-child policy.

Consequences for Chinese society are also deeply significant. The sex ratio at birth increased significantly (from 108 males per 100 females in 1980, slightly above the natural observed ratio, to 114 males per 100 females in 2014), and China had 33 million more men than women in 2014. This imbalance creates difficulties for the younger generation to form couples and to get married. Family relationships are also very important in China and used to be based on extended families, while they are now typically made up of nuclear families centred on a "little emperor" cherished by two parents (themselves single children) and four grand-parents. Anthropological transformations of kinship are therefore tremendous. The dependency ratio (measuring the ratio between the dependent young and old, and the working age population) is growing

---

42. Quanbao Jiang; Shuzhuo Li and Marcus W. Feldman, "China's Population Policy at the Crossroads: Social Impacts and Prospects", *Asian Journal of Social Science*, Volume 41, Issue 2, pages 193 – 218, 2013. https://www.ncbi.nlm.nih.gov/pmc/articles/PMC4657744/, accessed March 3, 2018. http://fortune.com/2015/11/02/china-one-child-policy/, accessed March 3, 2018;

43. White (Martin King), Feng (Wang), Cai (Yong), "Challenging Myths About China's One-Child Policy", *The China Journal*, no. 74. 1324-9347/2015/7401-0008. Pp. 144-159. Copyright 2015 by The Australian National University.

since 2014. No doubt, a large aging population increasingly dependent on younger generations will have deep economic and sociological impacts. On a more positive tone, one-child baby girls receive better consideration in Chinese families and society today that they did in the past, in particular a better access to education. However, many of these young girls are hidden children without legal registration and remain severely discriminated in access to health and education services.[44] Above all, the incalculable number of abandoned baby girls unable to survive is a massive denial of their right to life, and a deadly instance of gender discrimination for what Amartya Sen called "the missing women" of China.[45]

On October 29, 2015, the Chinese government announced that the existing law would be changed to a two-child policy. The new law became effective on January 1, 2016, following its passage in the standing committee of the National People's Congress on December 27, 2015.

Figure 2: Total Contraception Procedures in China, 1971-2011

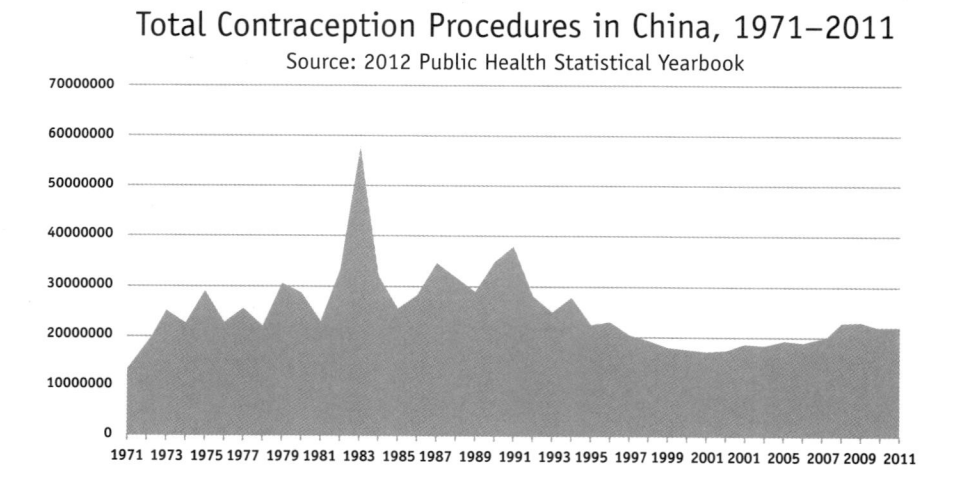

44. Johnson (Kay Ann), *China's Hidden Children. Abandonment, Adoption, and the Human Costs of the One-Child Policy.* The University of Chicago Press, 2016.
45. Sen (Amartya), "More than 100 Million Women are Missing". *The New York Review of Books*, 1990, December. http://www.nybooks.com/articles/1990/12/20/more-than-100-million-women-are-missing/

Figure 3: Contraception Procedures in China by Types, 1971-2012

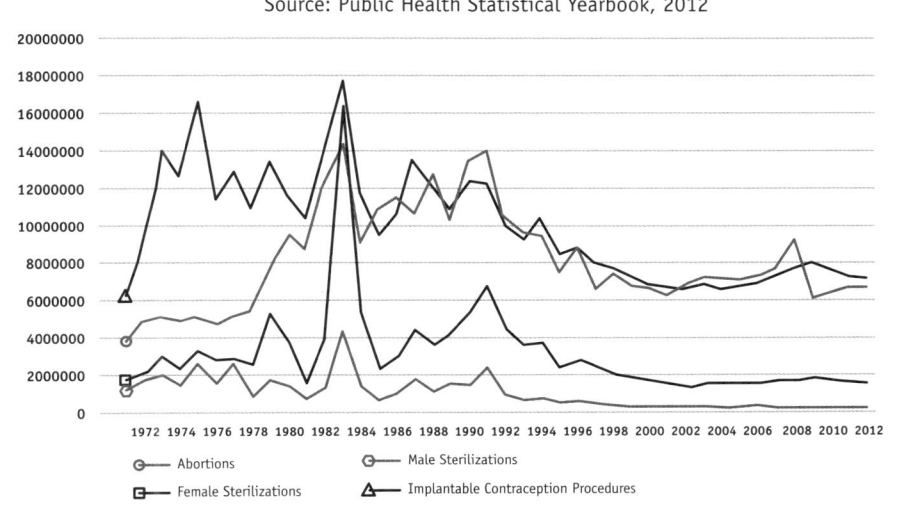

Figure 4: Contraception Procedures in Guangxi, 2003-2012

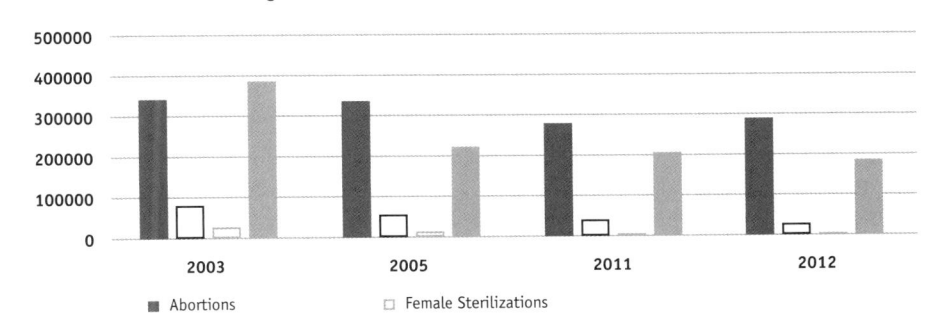